Finding Freedom

The Business Owner's Guide to Building a
Valuable Company and a Meaningful Life

FOREWORD BY BO BURLINGHAM

Jean Moncrieff

Small Giants
PRESS

Published by Maison Vero
1619 Providence Rd., Ste 220-254
Marvin, NC 28173

Inquiries may be directed to: Maison Vero, 1619 Providence Rd., Ste 220-254 Marvin, NC 28173, or info@graymilleragency.com.

For information about special discounts for bulk purchases, please call 1-949-333-4872 or email info@graymilleragency.com.

Maison Vero is a partner brand of The Gray + Miller Agency, a speaking, literary, and talent consortium.

For more information on the talent represented by The Gray + Miller Agency, or to bring any of our thought leaders to your organization or live event please visit our website at graymilleragency.com

Cover Design: Michael Elwell
Illustrations: Bogdan Apalaghiei
Book Design: Mel Wise

Manufactured in the United States of America

Paperback: 978-1-969508-31-8   E-book: 978-1-969508-33-2
Hardcover: 978-1-969508-32-5

Jean offers a thoughtful reminder that great companies are built from the inside out. *Finding Freedom* encourages leaders to reflect on who they are, what they stand for, and how to build organizations that create real and lasting value.

—Paul Spiegelman
cofounder, Small Giants Community and Kintsugi Village

In a world full of business books that tell you what to do, *Finding Freedom* goes deeper; it asks why you're doing it in the first place. The chapters on intentional growth and purpose alone are worth the price of the book. Whether you're just stepping into leadership or have been in the seat for decades, this book will challenge you in the best possible way.

—Eric Rieger, founder and CEO of WEBIT Services, Inc.

Finding Freedom has the makings of a small-business bible. Jean Moncrieff has written a rare kind of guide—one that blends compelling stories, sharp analysis, and practical advice owners can actually use. It's a book for leaders of stuck companies who want to regain momentum, but it's also the kind of book you'll return to again and again as new challenges arise. What gives it real power is that Jean has lived every lesson he shares. His honesty about his own journey gives this book an authority—and humanity—that most business books lack.

—Loren Feldman, founder of 21 Hats Media

The world is full of daring entrepreneurs who were once filled with purpose and passion, who now feel trapped and even embittered by the personal sacrifices they have had to make. In this transformative book, Jean Moncrieff brilliantly reveals how business owners can build and scale a valuable business, and find the freedom to exit without sacrificing the purpose, culture, and impact of what they spent most of their lives building.

—Davin Salvagno, #1 bestselling author of *Thieves of Purpose*

Jean's style is direct, succinct, and credible. He shares his own mistakes and failures. I recommend this book to both later and early stage companies. For new founders, this provides a roadmap and non-obvious goals to consider.

—Carl Erickson, founder and CEO (retired) of Atomic Object

In memory of my father, Michael John Moncrieff.
You lit the spark that became my entrepreneurial journey,
and your support never left me—even after you did.

Thanks, Dad. I miss you every day.
I only wish you could have been here to see this book come to life.

Table of Contents

Foreword ix

Introduction 1

Part One: Intentional Growth   9

Chapter 1:
What's Holding You Back? 11

Chapter 2:
The Perfect Storm 21

Chapter 3:
Getting Intentional About Growth 29

Chapter 4:
The Power of Purpose 41

Part Two: Growth Foundations   49

Chapter 5:
Laying the Groundwork for Transformative Growth 51

Chapter 6:
Choosing a Clear Three-Year Destination 61

Chapter 7:
Building a High-Performing Leadership Team 79

Chapter 8:
Your Execution Engine 89

Chapter 9:
Mastering Your Cash System 97

Chapter 10:
Investing in People Worth Building With 109

Part Three: Creating Value   121

Chapter 11:
Understanding Value Creation 123

Chapter 12:
Customer at the Center 129

Chapter 13:
Dig a Moat ... 143

Chapter 14:
Be Switzerland ... 157

Chapter 15:
Create Recurring Revenue Streams ... 169

Part Four: Succession ... 181

Chapter 16:
The Succession Challenge ... 183

Chapter 17:
Clarify Your Number, and Your Why ... 197

Chapter 18:
The Evolving Exit Landscape ... 209

Chapter 19:
Traditional Exits and Their Place in the Journey ... 219

Chapter 20:
Your Exit Team and Timeline ... 229

Chapter 21:
Life After Exiting ... 237

Conclusion:
Crafting a Legacy of Freedom and Purpose ... 249

Gratitude ... 251

About the Author ... 253

Foreword

When I first set out to write *Small Giants*, I wasn't trying to start a movement. I was trying to answer a question that had been bothering me for years.

In the early days of my career at *Inc.* magazine, I had the chance to observe a number of remarkable companies. They had energy, personality—what I came to call mojo. You wanted to be associated with them. You wanted to work there, buy from them, be part of what they were building.

And yet, over time, many of those companies lost it.

They grew. They became successful by conventional measures. But somewhere along the way, they lost the very qualities that had made them special.

That's what led me to write *Small Giants*.

I wanted to understand why some companies were able to hold onto that mojo while others couldn't. What I discovered was that the difference came down to a choice. The companies that endured had decided—very deliberately—that they were going to define success on their own terms. They chose to be great instead of big.

That decision wasn't always easy. In fact, it often meant turning down opportunities, resisting pressure, and going against the prevailing wisdom of the time. But it allowed them to build businesses with strong cultures, deep relationships, and a clear sense of purpose—businesses that people cared about.

What I didn't anticipate was how deeply that idea would resonate.

Over the years, *Small Giants* became more than a book. It became a way for like-minded leaders to find each other—to connect around a shared belief that business can be both successful and meaningful. That belief gave rise to the Small Giants Community, which continues to grow and evolve in ways I never could have planned.

Jean Moncrieff's work is a natural extension of that idea.

If *Small Giants* was about recognizing that there is another way to build a business, this book is about what it takes to do it—intentionally. Because the truth is, most businesses don't lose their way all at once. It happens gradually, as decisions get made without a clear sense of direction or purpose.

What Jean brings to this conversation is both clarity and experience. He understands what happens when growth becomes the goal rather than the result. And he makes a compelling case for stepping back and asking a different question: *what are you actually trying to build?*

That question sits at the heart of every small giant.

The companies I wrote about had a clear answer. They knew who they were. They understood what mattered to them. And they made decisions—sometimes very difficult ones—to stay aligned with that.

This book carries that idea forward, offering a practical lens on how to build a business that creates value not just financially, but for the people inside it and the communities around it.

As I step back from my role in the Small Giants Community, I do so with a great deal of confidence.

Jean is now leading that community forward. He understands what makes these companies special, and more importantly, what it takes to sustain that over time. He has my full and enthusiastic support.

The idea of *Small Giants* has always been about choice—about deciding what kind of company you want to build and having the discipline to stay true to it.

This book is an invitation to make that choice with intention.

—Bo Burlingham

Publishers note: During the completion of this work, Bo Burlingham graciously offered to write the foreword to this book, but was unable to finish it due to health matters. The foreword included in this work is a combination of interviews with Bo, and personal messages exchanged between Bo and Jean.

Introduction

Midway across the Atlantic, suspended somewhere between London and New York, I peeled myself out of my seat and made my way to the bathroom.

I couldn't sleep.

I closed the door, locked it, and caught my reflection staring back at me in the mirror.

From the outside, it probably looked like success.
Growth. Opportunity. Momentum.
A South African building a global business.

Yet standing there, alone at 35,000 feet, I remember thinking: *What the hell am I doing?*

That moment wasn't burnout.
It wasn't failure. It was a realization.

A quiet tipping point where I began to sense that the business I was building (successful by every external measure) was no longer aligned with the life I thought it was meant to support.

I didn't act on it immediately. Most of us don't. But looking back, that was my freedom moment.

Why You're Here

Entrepreneurial freedom—to choose how you spend your time, create lasting value, and step away from the business on your own terms. That's the dream, right?

Most entrepreneurs don't set out chasing freedom in the same way. Some of us stumble into entrepreneurship, accidentally called to solve a problem or serve a need. Some are driven by purpose. Others by curiosity or ambition. And some simply want to work on their own terms.

The challenge is that freedom doesn't happen by accident. It takes intention. It takes clarity. And it takes the courage to do things differently—to lead with purpose, to build a team that can thrive without you at the center, and to shape a culture that reflects who you are and what you stand for.

Where many business owners struggle isn't because they lack capability or drive. It's because, in the noise of day-to-day operations, long-term vision fades. Culture gets diluted. The plan gets postponed. And instead of growing with clarity, the business slowly becomes more complex, more demanding, and more dependent on the owner.

This book exists for anyone who recognizes that tension.

Whether you built your business from scratch or stepped into a family company.
Whether you feel energized or exhausted.
Whether you're early in the journey or well into it.

If you're beginning to wonder what the next chapter should look like—and how to move forward without losing yourself in the process—you're in the right place.

My Story

In the late '90s, I cofounded a web content management startup that grew quickly and attracted serious interest. But ego and inexperience got in the way. When the dot-com bubble burst, so did our future.

Years later, I built a group of information management companies that generated eight-figure revenues. From the outside, things looked great. Inside, I was exhausted. Overextended. At the center of everything.

Despite its size, the business had little value without me. I had chased growth without building something sustainable. No strong systems. No true leadership team. No clear intention. Just the single-minded pursuit of revenue.

When it came time to sell, I discovered the business wasn't worth what I thought.

It was around that time that I found myself staring at my reflection in the bathroom window midway across the Atlantic.

I could walk away, or I could transform the business into something valuable. I chose transformation.

Success doesn't come from pushing harder. It comes from looking in the mirror. From a shift in mindset. Like many business owners mentioned in this book, I had reached a tipping point.

Fortunately, I wasn't alone. I was part of a community of business owners who supported me through that transition.

Eventually, I sold the business and moved on to the next chapter. But more importantly, I found something far more valuable than an exit. I found a new sense of purpose and with that the freedom I so desired.

WHY THIS BOOK IS IMPORTANT

Since then, I've worked with hundreds of business owners who've reached a similar crossroads—sometimes feeling stuck or exhausted, sometimes simply unsure how to move forward.

Today, I lead the Small Giants Community, a global group of purpose-driven, values-based leaders who've chosen to run their companies differently. They prioritize people over short-term gains, culture over convention, and long-term impact over quick wins.

From that vantage point, I've begun to see something bigger emerging—something that goes beyond any one business or leader.

We are entering a period of profound transition. From where I sit, three forces are converging forces that will reshape leadership, business, and the economy over the next decade:

- **A Next-Gen Leadership Crisis:** Fewer than one in five companies have the bench strength they need to fill critical roles.[1] Nearly 10,000 Baby Boomers reach retirement age every day, yet incoming Gen X and Millennial leaders haven't been adequately prepared for the responsibilities headed their way.

- **The Silver Tsunami:** From 2024 through 2027, more than 4 million Americans will turn 65 each year—the largest aging wave in U.S. history. By 2030, every Baby Boomer will be 65 or older, accelerating turnover and reshaping the workforce at unprecedented speed.

- **A Forecasted Economic Downturn:** ITR Economics predicts a major depression around 2030.[2] Even if the timing shifts, the message is clear: turbulence is coming, and only organizations with strong culture, clear purpose, and resilient leadership will withstand it.

Most business owners are focused on getting through the next quarter. Few have the space to lift their heads and look at what's forming on the horizon. Yet now, more than ever, that broader perspective matters.

What gives me hope is what I see inside the Small Giants Community. When owners realign around purpose, build trust in their teams, and release the need to control everything, the shift is tangible. Less stress. More momentum. Businesses that don't just perform better but feel better to lead.

That's why I wrote this book.

---

1   Team Stage *Leadership Statistics: Demographics and Development 2024* (2024), https://teamstage.io/leadership-statistics/#leadership-training-statistics-benefits-effectiveness-and-styles, accessed December 6, 2025

2   ITR Economics, *Your Guide to Success Through the 2030s* (2024), https://promotions.itreconomics.com/hubfs/GD_eBook_2024.pdf, accessed December 6, 2025

Not just to share tools and frameworks (though you'll find plenty) but to address a moment of urgency for entrepreneurs. We start businesses in search of freedom, yet too often we become the constraint that prevents the business from becoming what it's capable of being.

And that's a problem, because small businesses matter more than ever.

They create jobs. They sustain communities. They have the power to make a meaningful dent in the world. But only if they're built to endure.

As we navigate a period of economic, leadership, and generational transition, this kind of growth can't be accidental. It requires awareness. It requires intention. And it requires leaders who are willing to look in the mirror and choose a different way forward.

This book is written for that moment.

THE PROBLEM STARTS AT THE TOP

Here's the good news. And the hard truth.

You are not the sole driver of your company's success. But when too much depends on you, the business can only grow so far. This mindset doesn't just stall the business. It becomes a self-fulfilling prophecy.

Sometimes that means letting go of trying to be the smartest person in the room. Sometimes it means stepping back from the day-to-day. But always, it requires honest self-reflection and the courage to evolve.

As the title of Marshall Goldsmith's enduring book famously saiy, "What Got You Here Won't Get You There."[3] The most important word in that phrase: *you*. Because, as the old saying goes: a fish rots from the head down. And while that might sound harsh, transformational change starts with you.

---

3   Marshall Goldsmith and Mark Reiter, *What Got You Here Won't Get You There: How Successful People Become Even More Successful* (New York: Grand Central Publishing, 2007).

WHO THIS BOOK IS FOR

This book is for business owners and entrepreneurs.

You've built a good business, and you sense it has the potential to become something even greater.

It's for owners who want to build a business that is valuable, not just busy. A business that creates options, not obligations. A business that can grow, endure, and adapt, even as your role within it changes.

It's also for leaders who recognize that the health of the business is inseparable from the mindset of the person at the top, and that how you lead, decide, and show up shapes everything that follows.

Throughout the book, we return to a simple, often uncomfortable idea: the greatest opportunity for creating value usually begins with greater self-awareness.

Because businesses that endure are built by leaders who understand themselves, build capable teams, and design organizations that don't rely on heroics to succeed.

Wherever you are on your entrepreneurial journey, the questions in this book matter. The earlier you engage with them, the more intentional and flexible your path forward can be.

What's Inside the Book

This book is divided into four parts, each reflecting a key stage in the entrepreneurial journey toward greater freedom. Each section builds on the one before it—starting with intention, moving through foundations and value creation, and culminating in readiness for transition.

Whether you're early in your journey or well into it, you can engage with the parts that feel most relevant right now. Over time, they're designed to work together, helping you build a business that creates real options for both the company and for you.

Part One: Intentional Growth

We begin with clarity. What do you really want? What's pulling you forward, not just as a business owner, but as a person? This section focuses on aligning growth with purpose, so the business is moving in a direction that actually matters to you.

Part Two: Growth Foundations

Growth without intention is a trap. Here, we focus on the foundations that support sustainable progress: leadership, people, systems, and alignment. The goal isn't growth for its own sake but building a business that can scale without relying on you at the center of everything.

Part Three: Creating Value

Freedom comes from building something others would value—even if you never plan to sell. This section explores how to create a business that is durable, transferable, and less dependent on you, by strengthening the core drivers of long-term value.

Part Four: Succession

The final section focuses on readiness. Whether succession is years away or closer than you expect, we explore how to prepare (strategically and personally) so that when the time comes, you have choices and can move forward on your own terms.

But before we dive into strategies and frameworks, we need to address the fundamental question: are you ready to transform not just your business, but yourself?

Part One: Intentional Growth

Before we talk about how to grow your business, we need to pause and look at how you're leading it.

Part One of this book is about stepping back and seeing what's really going on. Sometimes we're so consumed with achieving our short-term goals that we forget to step back and look at the bigger picture. Over time, that narrow focus can quietly pull us deeper into the business. We lose sight of our original intent and long-term direction, and before we realize it, we're operating in the weeds rather than leading the business toward its vision.

The chapters in this section are designed to help you notice patterns, not judge them. To reflect, not react. You don't need all the answers yet and you don't need to act immediately. This part of the book is about awareness and alignment. It's about getting clear on what you're growing toward and why.

If Part One does its job, you'll start to see your role differently. You'll recognize where intention has drifted, where growth has created complexity instead of freedom and where a clearer direction could change how decisions get made.

Everything that follows in this book builds on that shift.

So, take your time here. Read with curiosity. Notice what resonates. We'll get to the foundations and the structure soon enough.

For now, this is about setting your intention.

CHAPTER 1:
What's Holding You Back?

"Two young people I hoped would lead the future of the company came to my desk and said, 'If you don't change, we're leaving.' And I couldn't afford to lose them."

—Tom Walter,

Founder and chief culture officer, Tasty Catering

Entrepreneurs and leaders are wired for control. We like being at the wheel. We'd rather push through resistance than slow down and ask for help, or worse, admit we might be wrong. That grit and determination are what get businesses off the ground in the first place.

I know, because I was very good at that part.

Inspired by Sir Richard Branson and his book *Screw it, Let's Do It*,[4] I set out to build a group of information management companies across sub-Saharan Africa. In the early years, it worked. I quickly scaled the business, acquired a competitor, expanded into document imaging, bought a document storage business, and negotiated master reseller rights with multiple technology vendors.

From the outside, it all looked fantastic.

But the very qualities that drove my initial success—being hands-on, making every decision, solving every problem—eventually became the things that held me back. Instead of building something scalable, I had stacked a house of cards waiting for a strong enough gust of wind.

---

4   Richard Branson, *Screw It, Let's Do It: Lessons in Life and Business* (London: Virgin Books, 2010).

What was missing soon became painfully obvious:

Focus. Systems. Alignment. Leadership.

I was strong on ideas and galvanizing people around a cause. I could take something from zero to a couple of million. I could cobble business together into something much bigger. But I struggled to build the foundations required to scale—a high-performing, aligned leadership team, a clear strategy, and an execution system that didn't rely on me.

Instead, I became obsessed with revenue growth. I was always chasing the next opportunity: another acquisition, a new partnership, a new product, a new market. Complexity increased, but the leadership depth and execution discipline didn't keep pace.

This is how leaders end up in what I call *Growth Purgatory*. The business doesn't collapse (not at first), but it doesn't truly progress either. It can sit there for years—sometimes decades—until the owner finally wakes up to the problem, or the strain causes the whole thing to tip over and the eject button starts to look appealing.

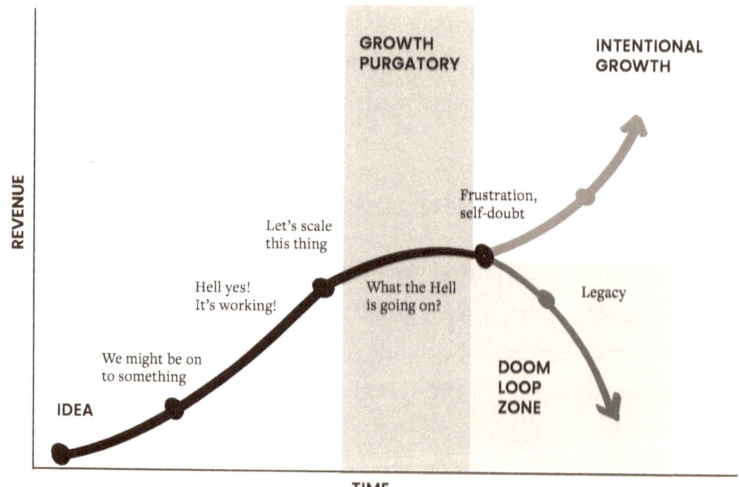

It took me years to see it clearly. I was the right person to start the business. I held the vision. But I wasn't the right person to scale it, at least not alone. And instead of surrounding myself with people who challenged me, I surrounded myself with people who adapted to me.

Those who stayed learned how to work around my leadership style. Those who didn't took their talent elsewhere.

It wasn't until I hit the eject button and chose to sell the business that the lesson truly landed: real value is created when you let go of control and build a business that can thrive without you at the center.

Three Ways Owners Get Stuck

Over the years, through my own experience and through coaching hundreds of business owners, I've noticed a pattern. Most stuck entrepreneurs don't lack ambition, intelligence, or work ethic. They tend to get caught in a limiting leadership style. The three that I see most often include:

THE COMMANDER

The Commander leads through decisiveness and control. Standards are high. Accountability is clear. In the early days, this works exceptionally well.

But as the business grows, command-and-control becomes a constraint. Decisions bottleneck. People wait to be told what to do. And leadership capacity never develops because there's no space for it to emerge.

Tom Walter lived this.

At one-point, Tasty Catering was facing debt, internal conflict, and a culture that was beginning to unravel. Tom was leading the way he always had—directing, correcting, and carrying the weight himself—until two young leaders he hoped would shape the future of the company confronted him with an ultimatum: change, or they would leave.

That moment forced Tom to confront his leadership style. He let go of command-and-control. He listened. He empowered others. He stopped trying to be the smartest person in the room. I share more on Tom's story in the case study at the end of this chapter.

THE VISIONARY

This one is personal. It's my default style. I can paint the big picture and rally people around a purpose. But as you read in the previous section, I get distracted and start chasing the next shiny object.

Visionaries are driven by possibility. They see what could be. They create momentum. They open doors. They're energized by the future.

The trap is restlessness.

Once the business requires discipline, systems, and consistency, the visionary gets bored. Focus drifts. New ideas become distractions. Execution never quite stabilizes.

Daniel Priestley, award-winning entrepreneur and founder of Dent Global, described this candidly in a *Diary of a CEO* interview.[5] Around the $2 million mark, he noticed how his entrepreneurial energy and creativity—so effective in the startup phase—were now getting in the way. He found himself distracted, constantly chasing new ideas, and realized that scaling a company required a fundamentally different kind of leadership. That self-awareness, and the humility to act on it is rare but essential.

Dan has turned this into a strength. He now partners with leaders who are exceptionally good at taking a business from $2 million to $10 million and beyond, while he uses the platform to evangelize the mission and grow demand.

---

5   Simon Bartlett, "The Money Making Expert: The Exact Formula for Turning $100 into $100K Per Month! – Daniel Priestly", *The Diary of A CEO*, YouTube video accessed December 19, 2024.

THE TECHNICIAN

The Technician is the expert. The craftsperson. The one who knows how the work is done. In *The E-Myth Revisited*, Michael Gerber describes this as the "technical entrepreneur trap."[6] It's the point where a business built around personal expertise reaches a ceiling because the owner is still operating as the technician rather than the leader the business now requires.

At first, that ceiling is rarely caused by market forces or a lack of resources. More often, it's a mindset issue. The owner hasn't yet built—or doesn't yet know how to build—the leadership and systems to carry the business forward. Over time, what once felt like a strength becomes a liability. A deep focus on craft and quality turns into rigidity. When the industry evolves, the business doesn't move with it.

I've seen this pattern play out many times. Years ago, I worked with a company built around securing on-premises Microsoft Exchange Server environments. But as the cloud began to reshape the industry, customers moved faster than the owner was willing to move. The technology was shifting, but his mindset couldn't keep pace. Today, that company is a fraction of what it once was.

We're seeing the same dynamic emerge again with artificial intelligence (AI). Many owners are resisting the shift to an AI-driven world, even as their customers move ahead without them. Unless they evolve, their current value propositions are at serious risk of being eroded.

For leaders who identify strongly with their expertise, navigating these kinds of inflection points can be particularly difficult—not because they lack capability, but because change threatens the very thing that made them successful.

---

6   Michael Gerber, *The E-Myth Revisited: Why Most Small Businesses Don't Work and What to Do About It* (New York: Harper Business, 2004).

The Hard Question

No matter which pattern shows up most strongly for you, the underlying question is the same:

Am I the right person to scale this business toward my vision?

That question isn't an accusation. It's an invitation.

As you read this, notice which of these questions creates the most tension for you:

- Are you building a culture of genius or trying to be the genius?
- Are you clinging to control or empowering your team to lead?
- Are you so deep in the business that the bigger picture is starting to blur?

If one of these makes you uncomfortable, that's not a problem. Discomfort is often a signal that you're standing at the edge of growth.

For many business owners, this realization doesn't arrive with a bang. It shows up quietly—a frustrating lull, a key team member considering a departure, or the creeping sense that you've lost control of your time, or worse, the future of the business.

You're not alone. And you're not broken. But to move forward, something has to change.

Breaking the Cycle

Most businesses don't immediately fail. They stall.

They drift into *growth purgatory*. Busy, but not better. Always working, rarely moving forward. The symptoms surface as stalled momentum, disengaged employees, and frustration that no matter what you try, nothing seems to work.

Sometimes it takes a jolt to break the pattern—a key leader leaves, a major customer walks, or you wake up one morning and wonder whether any of this is worth it.

That's the moment of truth: double down on what's no longer working or change your mindset.

Tom Walter chose the latter.

CASE STUDY: TOM WALTER AND THE CULTURE REBUILD AT TASTY CATERING

When Walter moved Tasty Catering into a much larger facility, it should have felt like a turning point. Instead, it became a magnifying glass.

Walter had always led with a command-and-control style. He made the decisions. He set the direction. He expected people to follow. That approach had helped him build a successful business—but the move into a new facility came with significant debt, and the added pressure intensified everything.

As the stakes rose, so did the control.

Micromanagement increased. Authority replaced trust. The culture began to strain under the weight of decisions bottlenecked at the top. What had once been manageable was no longer sustainable.

Then came the moment that forced the issue.

Two young employees—his son Tim, and Tim's close friend, Jamie— walked into his office with a clear message: *If you don't change, we're leaving.*

They weren't just employees. Walter saw them as the future of the company. Losing them would have been devastating—especially at a moment when walking away from the business wasn't an option. The debt tied him to the company, and failure would have followed him for years.

Faced with that reality, Walter was forced to confront a hard truth: the leadership style that had helped him build the business was now holding it back.

Rather than doubling down, he chose to listen.

Jamie, Tim, and a third teammate, Erin, proposed a fundamental shift. The company would be rebuilt around **employee-defined values**, not owner-imposed rules. Leadership would move away from command and control toward shared accountability and trust.

To anchor the change, the team turned to Jim Collins' *Good to Great.*[7] The book became a common language across the organization—they purchased both English and Spanish editions so everyone could participate. Small teams met weekly in book clubs, discussing discipline, leadership, and long-term thinking. These ideas weren't abstract. They shaped how the company operated.

Over time, Tasty Catering adopted Collins' principles of **disciplined people, disciplined thought, and disciplined action**, along with a Big Hairy Audacious Goal (BHAG): *to become the most recognized and respected brand in their industry.*

Walter's role changed with the business. He stepped out of day-to-day control and became Chief Culture Officer. His focus shifted from directing work to protecting values—ensuring decisions, systems, and behaviors aligned with what the team had defined together.

The results were striking.

Engagement rose. Employee turnover fell to just 4 percent in an industry known for churn. Decision-making moved closer to the work. People were trusted to act within clear boundaries—what Walter calls "freedom and responsibility within a circle of discipline."

---

7   Jim Collins, *Good to Great: Why Some Companies Make the Leap...and Others Don't* (New York: Harper Collins, 2001).

Walter now refers to his organization as being run by "60 CEOs"—people who think, act, and lead with genuine ownership. Many went on to become partners or launch their own businesses, carrying those values with them.

The business grew from roughly $3 million into a group of companies generating more than $75 million in revenue.

But the real transformation wasn't financial. It was cultural.

By letting go of control, Walter didn't abandon leadership. He evolved it—and in doing so, created a business strong enough to grow without him at the center.

FREEDOM FACTORS

The aim of this chapter has been to invite you to pause.

To consider whether your business might be stuck in *growth purgatory*—not failing but no longer moving forward in a meaningful way. To understand the risks of staying there too long, and to see how other owners have navigated this stage of the journey.

In the next chapter, we'll explore *why* this happens so often—and the role mindset plays in keeping leaders stuck or helping them move forward.

For now, these Freedom Factors are simply a place to reflect.

1. LET GO OF CONTROL

Notice where you're still holding on. Not because it's required, but because it feels safe. What once protected the business may now be quietly limiting it.

2. SHIFT FROM HERO TO BUILDER

Are you trying to be the answer, or are you building a business where others can lead? Sustainable growth begins when leadership stops relying on heroics.

3. RECOGNIZE THE SHIFT

The patterns that created early success don't always support what comes next. Growth often requires noticing when the game has changed—and choosing to play it differently.

CHAPTER 2:
The Perfect Storm

*"A mind is like a parachute.
It doesn't work if it is not open."*

—Frank Zappa

I love this quote from Zappa. It reminds me how many hard lessons I might have avoided had I been more open and more curious, a value that I'm certain only really comes with age.

In the early days, I was obsessed with chasing the next opportunity, moving from one idea to the next. Well-meaning, smart people urged me to focus, define a niche, and build a team. I resisted. Firstly, new opportunity energized me, and secondly, I was convinced I knew best. Sir Richard Branson's motto, "Screw it, let's do it!," became my answer to opportunity.

Had I listened and opened my parachute sooner, things might have unfolded very differently.

Then again, you might not be reading this book.

When Everything Starts Spinning

You may recognize the feeling.

You're working harder than ever, but momentum has slowed. Every day feels like a grind. You wake up bracing for whatever problem might rear its ugly head (I dreaded looking at email). It feels easier to do things yourself than trust anyone else. You're exhausted, and somewhere deep down is a quiet, unsettling question: *is this still worth it?*

While only you can answer that question, I can tell you that the longer you leave it unanswered, the tougher it becomes to make a change.

In chapter 1, we explored how leadership style can land you in growth purgatory. This chapter looks at what happens when those forces are left unchecked. Pressure rises. External change accelerates. And leadership instincts that once served you well begin to work against you.

What follows isn't random. It's predictable.

Almost every stalled business I've worked with is caught in one or both of two reinforcing patterns. Glen Dall calls one the CEO Doom Loop.[8] Jim Collins describes a similar dynamic in *Good to Great*.[9] When these loops collide, they create a perfect storm, one capable of grounding even the most capable founder.

DOOM LOOP #1: REACTIVE LEADERSHIP AND OWNER OVER-DEPENDENCE

The first Doom Loop is fueled by overreliance.

As complexity increases, the business quietly starts to depend more and more on the owner. Problems escalate upward. Decisions bottleneck. People wait instead of lead. What feels like staying close to the business is often the early stage of something more dangerous.

You stop leading and start managing.

Your strategic altitude drops. Instead of shaping the future, you're pulled into today's fires. And because the business lacks sufficient leadership depth, staying there feels justified.

This is where reactivity takes hold and your energy is sapped.

---

8   Greg Dall, Sreekanth Seshadri, Maria Palumbos, and James Ninkovich, *The CEO Playbook: Navigating Fears, Unlocking Success* (2023), https://www.apexnorthcoaching. com/download-white-paper, December 6, 2025.

9   Collins, *Good to Great*.

Research by Dall and Apex North[10] shows that one of the most common frustrations CEOs experience is an excessive dependence on themselves, often driven by a lack of aligned, capable leaders across the business. People problems compound quickly. A-players become harder to attract. C-players consume disproportionate energy. Alignment frays. Accountability weakens. Execution suffers.

The irony is that the more this happens, the more indispensable you feel.

Fear creeps in. You get more involved. You delay hard-people decisions. You tell yourself you will delegate once things stabilize, unaware that this pattern is preventing stability from arriving. Nearly 40 percent of CEOs surveyed cite fear of failure as their dominant concern, and most of those also question whether they truly have what it takes to lead at the next level.

Recall the software company from chapter 1. As the cloud reshaped the market, the signals were clear but inconvenient. Customers shifted. The team raised concerns. The data was undeniable. Instead of adapting, the founder tightened control and doubled down on what had always worked. Revenue stalled. A-players left. The culture eroded.

It wasn't a lack of intelligence that held him back. It was fear of the unknown, reinforced by ego.

In Dall's Doom Loop, the leadership system organizes itself around the owner.

And the longer the system runs that way, the harder it becomes to escape the Doom Loop.

DOOM LOOP #2: SHINY OBJECT SYNDROME

When results disappoint and pressure mounts, many business owners begin to **lose focus on what matters most and get sucked in perceived opportunities.**

---

10   Dall, et al, *The CEO Playbook.*

Rather than slowing down and returning to fundamentals, they begin searching for answers anywhere they can find them. New ideas surface. New initiatives are launched. New opportunities appear. Few are fully understood, tested, or connected by a coherent strategy.

In *Good to Great*, Collins describes this as the Doom Loop—the opposite of the Flywheel effect. Instead of building momentum through disciplined thought and consistent action, organizations react to setbacks by impulsively changing direction. Each disappointing result triggers another shift, another opportunity, another bet.

This is where shiny object syndrome takes hold.

Energy moves away from fueling the Fly Wheel and toward chasing possibilities. Products and services are introduced with minimal research. Initiatives are launched because they *might* work, not because evidence suggests they will. Activity replaces insight, with the hope that the latest gamble will create momentum.

It rarely does.

Collins contrasts this behavior with great companies, which resist the urge to lurch. When performance falters, they don't panic. They seek understanding. They listen more closely to customers. They refine their strategy. And they keep pushing the Flywheel in one clear direction.

The software company followed the Doom Loop path. Rather than committing to a disciplined transition toward cloud-based security, the founder chased opportunistic product ideas aimed at the existing customer base. Each new idea was framed as the breakthrough idea the company needed to change its fortune. None of them gained any traction.

Resources were drained. Focus fragmented. Trust eroded.

This is the cruel irony of the Doom Loop. In trying to escape stagnation, leaders create more of it. Not by choosing the wrong direction, but by abandoning direction altogether.

The Perfect Storm

When these two loops collide—reactive leadership and shiny object syndrome—you have the makings of a perfect storm:

- You ignore external signals
- You cling to familiar instincts
- You chase ideas without anchoring them to purpose
- You lose your best people and your strategic grip

Like an inexperienced pilot flying into what looks like harmless cloud cover, you enter danger without realizing it. Visibility drops. Instincts mislead. And the more you manipulate the controls, the worse the situation becomes.

Flying Blind: Trust Your Inputs

Imagine flying a small plane into a dense cloud.

You cannot see the horizon. Your brain tells you you're climbing when, in fact, you're descending. Panic urges you to pull, turn, *do something*.

Experienced pilots are trained to ignore those instincts. Instead, they trust their instruments.

I know this because I learned my lesson the scary way.

During a solo training flight, I deliberately flew into clouds, curious about spatial disorientation. Within seconds, I lost situational awareness. Panic set in. The only way out was to force myself to look down and trust my instruments, even as every instinct screamed otherwise. Had I followed my instincts, I could have stalled the aircraft and slipped into a spin.

Business works the same way.

When you're flying blind, ignoring input from the external environment, it's easy to drift into one or both Doom Loops. I see this constantly: owners dismissing customer feedback or teams too afraid to share what they're really hearing in the market.

Like pilots, business owners need reliable instruments to navigate complexity. Customer feedback. Market data. Financial trends. Honest feedback from people closest to the market. When uncertainty rises and situational awareness drops, those signals aren't optional. They're essential.

And just like in the cockpit, things get dangerous when you ignore external inputs.

Building Situational Awareness

A friend of mine, Tony, flies the Airbus A380 for Emirates. Every six months, he spends hours in a simulator—practicing abnormal system failures, adverse weather scenarios, and emergency procedures. The stakes are too high to rely on instinct alone.

Most entrepreneurs face complexity every day with far less training and far more arrogance.

To grow a business, you must deliberately build situational awareness:

- Commit to ongoing learning with coaches and peers who challenge you
- Replace assumptions with data
- Create upward visibility so your team can speak honestly
- Adapt early, before drift becomes danger

This isn't a one-time reset. It's a new way of leading.

From Closed Loop to Open Mindset

The founder of the software company clung to what he knew, dismissing feedback and resisting change. That is what a closed mindset looks like in action. And it's the fuel that keeps the Doom Loops spinning.

Now contrast that with Richard Bryan.

CASE STUDY: RICHARD BRYAN'S TURNAROUND

When Richard Bryan inherited his family's $120 million automotive business, it was already deep in crisis. The company carried a $5 million overdraft, had just lost $3.5 million, and employed 360 people—many protected by tenure rather than performance or customer focus.

At 28 years old, Richard lacked the experience—and the credibility—to turn things around on his own. Instead of pretending otherwise, he made a decisive move: he brought in a mentor.

Frank, a 58-year-old ex-special-forces officer with a reputation for bold turnarounds, didn't advise from a distance. For over two years, he worked alongside Richard, sharing an office, making decisions, and executing relentlessly.

Early moves were hard. They closed a failing truck dealership. Seventy roles were eliminated. Cash was freed. Trust with the bank restored.

Frank's rule was simple: *"We're going to make decisions every day, and if we get more right than wrong, we'll win."*

They introduced open-book management, rebuilt trust through radical transparency, and replaced ten out of twelve senior leaders. A-players rose through the ranks. Culture shifted. Short meetings, stand-ups, and clear communication became the norm.

The results followed. Customer satisfaction jumped from 250th nationally into the top ten. Profitability returned. Over the next decade, Richard bought out fourteen family shareholders and eventually sold the business—knowing its value no longer depended on him.

He didn't escape the storm by working harder.

He changed altitude. Trusted the instruments. Built an A-player team. And let go of the need to be the hero.

FREEDOM FACTORS:

1. BUILD AND TRUST YOUR INSTRUMENTS

When complexity rises, instinct becomes unreliable. Replace gut feel with evidence. Build clear feedback loops from customers, markets, financials, and your team—and learn to trust them, especially when they challenge your assumptions.

2. CHOOSE DISCIPLINE OVER DESPERATION

When results disappoint, resist the urge to lurch. Don't chase shiny solutions or quick fixes. Slow down. Return to fundamentals. Focus on what truly drives value for your core customer and commit to consistent, disciplined action.

3. REGAIN STRATEGIC ALTITUDE

If everything requires your attention, nothing gets your leadership. Create space to step out of the reactive spin and see the whole system. Strategic altitude is where patterns emerge, trade-offs become clear, and direction is restored.

CHAPTER 3:
Getting Intentional About Growth

*"Intentional growth isn't about doing more.
It's about aligning your actions with your end goals
and focusing on what truly matters."*

—Ryan Tansom

After the turbulence of the last chapter, let's pause.

If you're still reading, something has already shifted. You've recognized that the problem isn't just the market, the team, or the timing. You've seen how capable, driven founders get pulled into patterns that slowly work against them. And you've probably felt a flicker of something uncomfortable but important:

This doesn't have to keep happening.

Chapters 1 and 2 were about awareness. About naming what's really going on and understanding why it's so common. This chapter is about orientation. About lifting your head, stepping out of the reactive spin, and asking a different question altogether.

Not *How do I fix this quarter?*
But *Where am I actually going?*

Most of us never slow down often enough to get intentional about what we are building—personally and professionally. Sure, you might run an annual planning session, set budgets, and define priorities. But how well do you connect those plans to a longer-term direction? How often do we revisit them once the year gets noisy?

A business doesn't become valuable by accident. It isn't built by chasing revenue or profit targets alone. It becomes valuable when it's built with intention—aligned to a clear direction, grounded in purpose, and designed to thrive without the owner at the center of everything.

What Are You Really Building?

If your business is not aligned with your life, it will eventually feel like a burden.

For many founders, the business slowly becomes their only purpose. It consumes time, energy, and identity. Other roles fade into the background: spouse, parent, friend, community member.

I'm reminded of Rick Moranis's character, Seymour, in *Little Shop of Horrors*. What starts as something small and oddly charming slowly turns into an insatiable creature. Seymour nurtures it, feeds it, reorganizes his life around it. And the more he gives, the more it demands.

"Feed me, Seymour! Feed me!"

Eventually, the plant threatens everything in Seymour's world. In the theatrical ending, he realizes the truth too late and is forced to kill the very thing he once believed would make his life better.

Many business owners recognize that moment. What began as a dream quietly turns into a monster that consumes their time, energy, and relationships. The difference is that in business, you don't get a dramatic finale. You just keep feeding the monster… and wondering why you're constantly exhausted.

And that's what happens when the future isn't clearly defined.

The business becomes your sole purpose.

But your purpose is bigger than your business alone, as Davin Salvagno explained when I interviewed him on *The Freedom Experience* podcast.[11] We all have many purposes. Our purpose as a parent, as a spouse, as a partner, as an entrepreneur. The question is whether your business supports them or crowds them out.

This is why intentional growth begins with life design and not business strategy.

Before asking *how* to grow, you must ask *what* you are growing toward.

- What kind of life do I want to live now and in the future?
- What role should my business play in that life?
- What outcomes would create real freedom?
- What other purposes in my life matter deeply and how do I protect space for them?

In the Small Giants Leadership Academy, we devote a whole module to visioning, purpose and creating a personal plan. This process ensures leaders are intentional about growth both personally and professionally.

Ten-Year Thinking

One of the disciplines I keep coming back to is something my friend Rob Dube leads with in his book *Shine: 10 Disciplines for Maximizing Your Energy, Impact, and Inner Peace.*[12] The very first discipline he introduces is **ten-year thinking**, and I love that he leads with it.

Ten years feels distant. Abstract. Uncertain.

That's precisely why it works.

---

11   Jean Moncrieff, "Thieves of Purpose: What's Really Holding You Back with Davin Salvagno," *The Freedom Experience with Jean Moncrieff,* YouTube video accessed November 16, 2025.

12   Gino Wickman and René Dube, *Shine: How Looking Inward Is the Key to Unlocking True Entrepreneurial Freedom* (Dallas: BenBella Books, Inc. 2024).

Thinking that far ahead stretches time. It slows urgency. It restores perspective. It pulls you out of reaction and into intention. As Dube describes it, when you think in ten-year timeframes, time slows down. You can see your priorities in the context of the big picture and you know where to put your focus and energy.

CREATE YOUR TEN-YEAR VISION

When I do this work myself, I use a two simple tools.

- One is a **One-Page Personal Plan** that captures my values, purpose, and ten-year vision.
- The other a **One-Page Company Plan** that summarize the vision for where the business is going.

But, before I get to these tools, I start with imagination. I spend time picturing what my life looks like ten years from now. I place myself in the future—almost as if I'm standing there looking back—and I write from that place: *this is what my life looks like. This is what the business looks like. This is how I'm showing up. This is what I'm building. This is what I've stopped doing. This is what matters now.*

It usually starts messy. Long-form journaling. Half-formed thoughts. Fragments. I just keep writing for thirty minutes. Then I step away. The following week, I pick up my scribbles and evolve them. I repeat the process until I've created a ten-year vision for where I want to be personally and professionally. Then I distil it into a few lines I can add to the vision section of my one-page personal plan.

Once the picture is clear, alignment becomes possible. I can see how it intersects with my business goals and be more intentional about building a business that actually supports the life I want to live.

We'll go deeper into building plans later in the book and I'll share these tools in the resources section at the end of the book. For now, what matters is this:

Long-term thinking eliminates chaos and urgency. Clarity about the future sharpens the focus of what you do in the present.

WORKING BACKWARD CREATES ALIGNMENT

From that ten-year picture, I can build the layers below it:

- What's my **ten-year goal**?
- What's my **three-year goal**?
- What do I want the next **twelve months** to look like?
- What matters most in the **next quarter**?

And I do this both personally and professionally.

On the personal side, I look at key areas of life—finance, family, faith, fitness, friends—and ask: ten years from now, how do I want to show up here? Who am I? What's strong? What's working?

Then I create a three picture. A one-year picture. And finally, my top three to five aligned priorities for the quarter.

On the business side, the questions are similar: where is the business going? What does it look like when it's valuable? When it's not dependent on me? When the team and systems are strong enough to carry it forward?

And then comes the real test:

What am I doing this quarter that actually moves me in that direction?

If your priorities and actions today aren't aligned with where you want to be in ten years, you're not building momentum.

FROM REACTING TO CHOOSING

In *The Science of Scaling*, Dr. Benjamin Hardy argues that unless you delib-erately frame the meaning of your past, your past will quietly drive your present.[13] Most people believe they are responding to circumstances. In reality, they are reacting to patterns they've never questioned.

We default to living from memory and urgency. The past becomes our reference point. The present becomes our pressure point.

But the future—the future is supposed to be the driver.

Hardy's central idea is simple: your present decisions should be shaped by the person you intend to become, not the person you have been.

That's where many owners get stuck personally and professionally. Instead of three-year vision of the future dictating what we do in the present, our past is dictating what we do... and keeping us stuck.

When a business feels heavy, the instinct is to look at what has worked in the past. To double down on it. To work longer. To chase whatever opportunity we see to gain momentum. And, in our minds, growth becomes synonymous with activity.

But approaching growth from the past is what has most companies trapped in growth purgatory—endlessly driving around the block, never really going anywhere.

Business owners end up stuck because they're operating inside a compressed time horizon. Quarters dominate thinking. Monthly numbers dictate emotion. And urgency crowds out vision.

And when your world shrinks to ninety days, everything feels chaotic.

This is why intentional growth begins with a mindset shift, not a plan.

Before deciding *how* to grow, you must decide *toward what*.

That requires shifting from being owner-operator to the owner—not reacting from the past or the pressure of the present, but making decisions from a clearly defined future.

---

13   Benjamin Hardy and Blake Erickson, *The Science of Scaling: Grow Your Business Bigger and Faster Than You Think Possible* (Carlsbad: Hay House Business, 2025).

The future you choose must become the lens through which you interpret today.

My Wake-Up Call

For years, I was obsessed with growth.

I scaled my business from $5 million to $20 million through partnership and acquisition. I was good at selling the vision. But while I was out painting the future, my employees were left bobbing in the wake of growth and cultural integration... or the lack of it.

Some had heard me talk about the big vision. Few, including myself, knew how we were actually going to get there.

Worse, I wasn't investing in the growth of my team or hiring leaders capable of taking us toward that vision. I needed people who knew how to scale a scrappy, cobbled-together group of companies into a $100 million business.

That was the dream.

But I wasn't building the foundation to support it.

I was an owner-operator, not a CEO. I wasn't shaping the business around what I wanted my life—or the company—to look like ten years into the future. I was trying to keep a house of cards from toppling while piling on more layers.

Until, on that flight home, it hit me:

This isn't what I signed up for.

The very thing I had built to give me freedom—the thing I had poured everything into—had become my own *Little Shop of Horrors*. I wasn't leading it anymore. I was feeding it.

Constantly. Endlessly.

Like Seymour, I could hear it: "Feed me, Jean! Feed me!"

I just wanted to walk out the door and never come back. I hadn't built a valuable business. I had created a monster that was sapping every ounce of energy from me.

That realization forced a shift.

I joined a group of founders and CEOs who were wrestling with similar questions about leadership and growth. I was introduced to open-book management, business operating systems, values-based decision-making, and the discipline of aligning daily action with long-term vision.

But more important than any framework, I found people who challenged my thinking and helped me open my mind. My parachute.

I stepped back. I brought in a coach. I set to work building a capable leadership team. We implemented a business operating system. We aligned around purpose. I delegated. I trusted. The weight lifted.

And slowly, the business began to operate without me at the center of it all.

The Owner-Operator Shift

When you don't choose your future, you default to operator mode.

You end up chasing short-term revenue and growth instead of a long-term vision. Expansion while still trying to control everything. You're deep in decisions, solving problems, holding the wheel tightly. The business may grow, but the foundations aren't there and ultimately, the strain begins to show.

The team waits for you.
Decisions bottleneck.
Energy gets scattered.

And before long you're being sucked into a Doom Loop—reacting instead of choosing, operating instead of designing.

Michael Gerber described this shift decades ago in *The E-Myth Revisited* when he talked about working *on* the business, not *in* it.[14] We've all heard it. Yet so many of us struggle to make that shift. Not because they don't understand it, but because stepping back feels like losing control.

But to truly control your business, you must begin to think like the CEO of your future business. You must be willing and open to evolving your mindset. To shift from an owner-operator mindset to an owner mindset. You must shift:

- From solving problems to recruiting problem solvers
- From chasing revenue to creating long term value
- From doing everything to building systems and leaders
- From living in the weeds to holding the bigger picture

This is how you begin to reclaim time, perspective, and choice.

Growth Starts with the Right People

Collins' "First Who...Then What" concept from *Good to Great* dictates that leaders must first get the right people on the bus, the wrong people off, and the right people in the right seats *before* determining where to drive the bus.[15]

This is where many founders and owners get it backward. They limp along with the wrong people on the bus. They make revenue and profit the purpose. They neglect culture and values. And the bus isn't pointed in the right direction.

As Walter (who you met in chapter 1) once told me, "When I started focusing on values, purpose, and culture, the revenue and profit followed."

That's the power of alignment. When you build a team that shares your values, when you define a clear vision, when you connect with your pur-

---

14   Michael Gerber, *The E-Myth Revisited: Why Most Small Businesses Don't Work and What to Do About It* (New York: Harper Business, 2004).

15   Collins, *Good to Great*.

pose—the business starts to grow for the right reasons. And the right people rally behind it.

CASE STUDY: DAVE'S MINDSET SHIFT AND HEALTHY GROWTH

Dave sat alone in the boardroom, staring at a whiteboard covered in half-finished plans and missed targets. It was late. Everyone else had gone home. But the pressure in his chest wouldn't let him leave.

"I was close to tears," he told me. "Like I'd tried everything... but nothing worked."

On paper, the business wasn't failing. But it had plateaued. Momentum had stalled. Every new initiative seemed to create more complexity instead of clarity. Dave was still carrying too much of the weight himself.

He was reacting, not choosing.

At a Vistage meeting, he heard someone speak about EOS—the Entrepreneurial Operating System. Something clicked. Not because EOS was a magic bullet, but because Dave realized he didn't have to carry everything alone.

He let go of needing all the answers.

He opened himself to support from an implementor. He recruited the strongest leadership team he could find. He reconnected with his values, his purpose, and the kind of company he wanted to build.

That's when things started to change.

For the first time, Dave wasn't just trying to fix the quarter. He was designing the future.

He shifted from owner-operator to owner and CEO.

He stopped reacting to pressure and began building structure. He stopped trying to be indispensable and began building capability. He stopped chasing momentum and began aligning around direction.

Today, Dave has a strong leadership team, a growing business, and time to spend with his family. But more importantly, he's building a company that reflects his values and vision—one that doesn't revolve around him but is better because of him.

An operating system played a role. But it wasn't EOS that changed Dave's business. It was a shift in mindset. He chose his future—and then built a company capable of reaching it.

FREEDOM FACTORS

1. CHOOSE YOUR FUTURE

Define the life and business you are building toward. Write it down. Make it concrete. If the future isn't clear, the past will keep driving your decisions.

2. LEAD FROM THE OWNER'S SEAT

Stop reacting to pressure and start making decisions from your ten-year vision. Shift from doing to designing. From solving problems to building people and systems that solve them.

3. BUILD INDEPENDENCE INTO THE BUSINESS

Identify where the business still depends on you and begin removing yourself from the center. Delegate authority, not just tasks. Create structure that allows the company to grow without your constant intervention.

CHAPTER 4:
The Power of Purpose

"What you do will only ever be as good as WHY you do it."

—Zach Mercurio

Purpose is Where the Shift Begins

Chapter 3 was about intention, lifting your gaze to see the bigger picture, and aligning current priorities with your future.

But vision and ten-year thinking alone are not enough.

You can have goals, plans, even momentum... and still feel like something is missing. You can grow revenue, add customers, hit targets—and still lose your best people if they don't feel connected to something meaningful.

That's because goals give you the destination.
Purpose tells you **why it matters.**

Bo Burlingham wrote about "the passion that leaders brought to what the company did" as one of the defining traits of a Small Giant.[16] Passion is that inward-focused feeling of enthusiasm for "what" you love doing. But more than passion, Burlingham describes how what set these companies apart was the extent to which a higher purpose was "woven into the fabric of the business." Purpose is the "why" that makes the work that people do meaningful. It continually reminds your people that what they do matters and why they should care about giving their best.

---

16   Bo Burlingham, *Small Giants: Companies That Choose to Be Great Instead of Big* (New York: Portfolio/Penguin, 2016).

Fifteen years ago, when the Small Giants Community first formed, there wasn't much hard evidence that purpose and people could materially impact the bottom line. Danny Meyer's "enlightened hospitality" was about all about creating an extraordinary experience customers couldn't get anywhere else—to bring them happiness. Entrepreneurs like Paul Spiegelman and Tom Walter were experimenting inside their companies with values, culture, and putting people first. But "purpose" still sounded like a fluffy waste of money to most business leaders.

Fast forward to 2026 and purpose is about as popular as "contains protein" is on a food wrapper. Which is a good thing I suppose, but still most business owners are as confused about purpose as they are about vision and mission statements.

Purpose connects the dots between what employees are doing daily and your company's higher purpose. That purpose might relate to the work your company does, or how you do it, or the impact your business makes in the world. It attracts and rallys people around a higher purpose, a cause greater than the business itself. Without purpose, it's easy to drift. You can be busy. Even profitable. But are you building something that matters—something that moves people and lasts?

Purpose marks a mindset shift from operating a business to **leading a mission**. From pushing harder to aligning everything around one meaningful aim.

Purpose Creates Alignment

Your Core Purpose is like a magnetic field. It attracts, it organizes, and it directs. It gives people a reason to care, a reason to contribute, and a reason to stay.

But here's the key: having a purpose isn't enough. You must be purposeful. That means leaders must show people *how* they matter—not just tell them that they do.

Zach Mercurio puts it bluntly: you can have a job that matters and still not experience *mattering* in your job.[17] The difference is leadership that connects people to purpose. People don't commit because you have a purpose statement. They commit when they can see how their work connects to a human outcome.

That's why NASA remains one of the best examples of purpose in action.

THE LADDER TO THE MOON

With over 300,000 contractors and technicians involved in the Apollo program, alignment could have been chaos. Most people knew their jobs would end when the mission ended.

And yet morale was high. Why?
Because NASA made the mission visible.

At facilities across the U.S., chalkboards displayed what became known as the "ladder to the moon."[18]

- At the top: land a person on the moon by the end of the decade.
- At the bottom: monthly tasks and team level goals.
- And on every rung between: a clear link between daily work and the mission.

This wasn't motivational fluff. It was a shared map.

That's why, when President John F. Kennedy asked a janitor what he did at NASA, the man replied: "I'm putting a person on the moon."

Mercurio describes purpose as the invisible leader: the force that guides decisions and behavior even when no one is watching. Instead of sticking your purpose up on the wall, consider having a seat at your leadership table

17   Zach Mercurio, *The Invisible Leader: Transform Your Life, Work, and Organization with the Power of Authentic Purpose*, (Seattle: Advantage Media Group, 2017).

18   Jean Moncrieff, "Episode 29: Zach Mercurio," *The Freedom Experience with Jean Moncrieff* (2024).

that represents your purpose. That way, at every leadership meeting, you and your team are asking: does this priority, this goal, this strategy, take us closer to our purpose?

Your Business Needs a Ladder

You may not be launching rockets, but you are building something that matters. And if you want your team to feel connected to that mission, you need to make the connection visible.

This doesn't require a workshop, a rebrand, or a three-month retreat. Although, it helps to bring in a coach who can help you through the process of defining your core purpose.

In the meantime, start by reflecting on your why: why it is you started the business in the first place? I suspect that if I asked the owner of the software security company I mentioned in the previous chapters, he'd tell me something like, "to protect small businesses from getting hacked." In the early days, it served him well. He attracted a bright team of people who rallied around the cause. But when the market shifted, the company lost sight of its purpose, and those clever people moved on.

This is why knowing and keep sight of your purpose is so important. Make the "why" easy for people to see and connect their everyday work to.

Here are a few prompts to sit with (not homework—just a starting point):

- What human outcome does this business create?
- Why did you start the business in the first place?
- Where do people lose sight of that outcome in the day-to-day?
- What story could you tell this week that reconnects the work to the mission?

When purpose becomes clear, alignment replaces control. Leaders gain freedom—not by working harder, but by letting purpose do the heavy lifting.

Finding My Purpose

To explain why this matters so deeply to me, I need to share where it became personal.

For a long time, I believed the purpose was building the business. Revenue. Growth. The eventual exit. For a while, that story worked. I scaled a company to $20 million, acquired other businesses, and said yes to every opportunity that came my way.

But somewhere along the line, the business became my identity.

I stopped showing up fully in my other roles—as a husband, a father, a friend. I was always chasing, always distracted. Eventually, it cost me my marriage. And it nearly cost me my health.

And if I'm honest, it's something I still have to keep in check today. I have a tendency to over-index on one mission—one passion—and that's never good.

After I sold the business (which I'll share more about later in the book), I hit a season where I felt unanchored. I invested in startups (never again). I helped business owners navigate their growth challenges. I even wrote a travel book (still unpublished). But I couldn't figure out what my purpose was and I drifted for a long time. Then something clicked: the work I was doing—the coaching, the mentoring, supporting other business owners, it wasn't just work.

It was calling me back to something deeper.

That's when I realized my purpose: *to create entrepreneurial freedom.*

Freedom for founders who feel trapped inside the businesses they built. Freedom for leaders who want to create something meaningful but don't know how. Freedom for myself, to live a life of alignment, adventure, curiosity, and contribution.

I didn't get there all at once. I'm not sure anyone ever does. Purpose isn't a destination—it's a North Star. Something you keep moving toward and trying to get better at fulfilling...even though you might never get there yourself. When I began reconnecting with what mattered most, everything started to change.

That's why I wrote this book. It's why I said yes to taking the torch at the Small Giants Community. Not because these things are easy, but because they connect with my purpose.

But for me, and perhaps for you too, I have to stay vigilant that my purpose as a business owner, leader, and entrepreneur enhances, not diminishes, the other purposes in my life.

CASE STUDY: CARL SAUNDERS AND THE POWER OF PURPOSE

Carl Saunders spent years leading Vorum, a company creating breakthrough prosthetics and orthotics technology. Yet despite strong products and hard work, the business plateaued at around **$5 million in annual revenue**, hovering in that range for years.

What made the plateau feel urgent wasn't just the number—it was the people. Carl had talented team members come to him and say some version of: "I like what we do here, but I can't see a future for myself if we don't grow." That was a turning point.

Not only was Vorum stalled, but it was at risk of decline. One by one, Carl's brightest team members started knocking on his door, saying the same thing: "I like working here, but I can't see a future for myself in this company."

Carl could've dismissed it. But instead, he made a shift. Through coaching, Carl and his leadership team clarified Vorum's Core Purpose: **to improve the quality of care for prosthetics and orthotics patients globally.** Then they made the purpose measurable. They began tracking their impact by how often a patient somewhere in the world was fitted using technology

Vorum enabled. At the time they first measured it, the number was about **one fitting every 120 seconds**.

That led to a bold, motivating goal: **one fitting every second.** Suddenly, the work wasn't just about revenue—it was about measurable impact. Purpose became a pull that helped align decisions, focus priorities, and energize the team. Carl describes a major shift in empowerment too moving from a world where he and his partner made roughly **95% of day-to-day decisions** to a company where, as they scaled, he was making **less than 5%**.

By the time Vorum was sold, their impact metric had improved dramatically: **one fitting every 62 seconds.** Carl's story is proof that purpose isn't fluff. When you make it real—and make it measurable—it becomes fuel.

Purpose isn't something you figure out once and move on from. It's the reference point everything else will now be built around. When clear, decisions simplify. Alignment replaces control. And the business stops pulling you in every direction at once.

This is the moment where clarity starts to shape decisions. In the chapters ahead, we'll translate that clarity into structure, rhythm, and systems that can carry the weight of growth. But before you move forward, anchor here—because everything you're about to build depends on it.

FREEDOM FACTORS

1. PURPOSE IS THE ANCHOR

Goals tell you where you're going. Purpose tells you why it matters—and why people should care enough to build it with you.

2. MAKE THE MISSION VISIBLE

Purpose becomes real when people can see how their work connects to a human outcome. Build your "ladder" one rung at a time.

3. LEAD PURPOSEFULLY

Purpose isn't a statement. It's a practice—modeled by the leader, reinforced through stories, decisions, and what you choose to prioritize.

Purpose won't fix everything overnight.

But it will give you and your team a reason to keep going. A reason to care. And a reason to grow.

In the next section, we'll move from mindset to structure, and lay the foundations for sustainable, scalable growth.

Part Two:
Growth Foundations

You've clarified what matters. Now we build. Part Two is where intention becomes infrastructure—where purpose shows up in meetings, metrics, roles, and rhythm. Sustainable growth doesn't happen by accident; it's designed through leadership, systems, alignment, and consistent execution. Whether you're steady, scaling, or stuck, the same principle applies: clarity must translate into structure. This section lays the foundations that allow your business to grow with discipline, confidence, and less dependence on you.

CHAPTER 5:

Laying the Groundwork for Transformative Growth

"By the time we sold the business,
I was pretty sure I was the dumbest person in the room—
and that's exactly where I wanted to be."

—Richard J. Bryan

Growth rarely stalls without reason.

When a business plateaus, it's easy to point to problems outside the business: the market has tightened, competitors have become more aggressive, customers are price-sensitive, the economy is uncertain. Sometimes those factors matter.

More often, however, the constraint sits inside the business itself.

Over the years, I've worked with companies across different industries—manufacturing, software, services, distribution. Different products. Different markets. Different leadership personalities. Yet when growth slows or momentum fades, the underlying causes tend to look remarkably similar.

Most stalled growth can be traced back to a small number of predictable barriers—issues that compound quietly over time until they begin to cap performance.

In my experience, those barriers fall into four categories:

1. Leadership
2. Market awareness
3. Systems and processes
4. People

These aren't abstract concepts. They show up in specific, practical ways. And until they are named and addressed, no strategy, however clever, will deliver the results you want.

This chapter is about understanding those barriers and how to overcome them as you start laying your foundation for growth.

Leadership: the Ultimate Constraint

In the early stages of a business, concentrated leadership is an advantage. The founder or cofounders make decisions. Communication is direct. Accountability is obvious. And decision making is driven by the need to survive.

But what accelerates early growth often limits growth down the line.

As companies scale, leadership must evolve from control to capacity. The business can no longer rely on one central decision-maker without creating friction. When every major decision, customer issue, or strategic choice flows through the owner, the organization slows, regardless of talent.

This doesn't happen because owners are incapable of delegating. It happens because they are competent. They know the product. They understand the customers. They've built the systems around themselves, and letting go feels risky.

Instead, they hire strong operators but retain final authority. They assemble leadership teams but don't fully empower them. Titles exist, but not ownership and authority.

Don't believe me? Take a moment to draw your organizational chart. Write down top tier functions: marketing, sales, finance, operations, development. How many of those roles are you ultimately accountable for now?

Most business owners are wearing multiple hats. The problem then becomes that:

- Decisions queue up
- Customers escalate upward (to you)
- 'Leaders' hesitate to act independently
- And you are the system

That model works under $1 million.
It creates a ceiling at $2 to 3 million.
And it's the reason your business is stuck in growth purgatory.

If you're wearing more than a couple of hats right now, building a leadership team should be your top priority. These aren't leaders who agree with everything you say. They're people capable of taking the business from where it is today toward your vision. They're talented and goal-oriented. They speak up and challenge one another—not because they need to be right, but because they're committed to the shared outcome. They own results, not tasks. And they're measured by impact, not proximity to the founder.

Richard Bryan understood this need when he stepped into his family's business, he made an early decision that changed the trajectory of the organization: he chose *not* to be the smartest person in the room.

Instead of doubling down on control, he brought in experienced leadership, sought counsel, and rebuilt the executive team over time. The transformation wasn't easy. People who had been with the organization for years had to be fired. But Richard didn't have a choice. He had to find help and make tough calls.

Growth and value creation followed.

The lesson is not that every business owner needs an interim turnaround executive. But being open to help makes a difference. The lesson is that what got you where you are won't get you to where you want to go. Growth requires a high-performing, cohesive leadership team, with the willingness and desire to grow and evolve.

Market Awareness: the Danger of Looking Inward

Operational excellence can become a blindfold.

I've seen companies with strong processes, disciplined reporting, and efficient operations gradually lose relevance because they were focused almost entirely inward. They optimized what they already did well while the market moved.

The warning signs are subtle:

- Customers mention new alternatives
- Frontline employees flag changing expectations
- Competitors experiment with different models

But leadership dismisses the signals. "Our customers don't want that." "It's a fad." "We tried something similar years ago."

This isn't arrogance as much as familiarity. Success reinforces existing assumptions. And the better a company is at executing its current model, the harder it can be to question that model.

Research from Chief Outsiders and the University of Texas McCombs School of Business found that companies led by operationally-focused CEOs often excelled at internal metrics but underperformed in growth compared to companies led by market-focused CEOs.[19] The difference wasn't intelligence. It was orientation.

Market-focused leaders maintain a disciplined habit of looking outward. They build feedback loops into leadership rhythms. They create structured conversations around customers, competitors, and trends.

One manufacturing CEO I worked with required each executive to bring one external insight to every leadership meeting—something observed in the field, heard from a client, or noticed in the market. That simple discipline shifted conversations from internal efficiency to external relevance.

Market awareness is not only a marketing function. It is a leadership posture.

When companies stop looking up, they drift. And drift, left unchecked, becomes decline.

Systems and Processes: the Backbone of Scale

In small organizations, clarity is informal. Everyone sits close together. Decisions are visible. Accountability is immediate.

Growth disrupts that simplicity.

As headcount increases, communication fragments. Priorities multiply. Handoffs become less obvious. Without deliberate systems, friction appears:

- Projects stall between departments

- Meetings expand but produce little resolution

- Accountability becomes shared and therefore diluted

---

19   Chief Outsiders and The University of Texas, McCombs School of Business, *Mid-Market CEO Study: Market-facing Companies Better at Converting Opportunities into Growth?* (2011), https://www.chiefoutsiders.com/hubfs/Mid-Market%20CEO%20Growth%20Study%20eBook%20-%20Rebranded_FNL.pdf accessed December 17, 2025.

Many founders resist formal systems because they associate them with bureaucracy. I did. I believed structure would slow us down or dampen entrepreneurial energy.

What I eventually learned is that the absence of systems does not preserve agility. It creates dependency.

Without clear processes, people escalate upward. Without visible priorities, teams guess. Without defined ownership, progress slows, even when everyone is working hard.

Years after I exited my business, I saw this from a different perspective.

My daughter, Courtney, got her first job at itsu, a fast-casual restaurant chain in the UK. She was sixteen. It was her first real experience of structured work.

On her first day, she wasn't simply handed a uniform and shown where to stand. She went through a defined onboarding process. She was given training and told how she could grow and progress in the organization. She was show how to assemble meals and pack shelves. She understood how the store opened, how it closed, how quality was maintained, and how performance was measured. Expectations were clear.

More importantly, she understood how she mattered and how she could progress.

She came home after her first week proud and energized. Not because the work was glamorous (she was assigned restroom cleaning duty her first week!), but because she had clarity. There were systems to follow. And she knew she her contribution mattered in creating a great experience for customers.

It reinforced in my mind how systems, when done well, are not restrictive. They are liberating.

They reduce ambiguity.
They accelerate competence.
They allow people to take responsibility sooner.

In my own business, we often operated on verbal instructions and improvisation. That worked when we were small. As we grew, the lack of formalized onboarding, documented processes, systems and structure created confusion that I mistook for "entrepreneurial flexibility."

In reality, I had become the system. Everything flowed through me.

And that is not scalable.

Well-designed systems do not remove ownership from people. They transfer it to them.

They make expectations visible.
They standardize what should be standard.
They free leaders to focus on improvement rather than firefighting.

When structure is missing, founders compensate. When structure is present, teams perform.

That is the difference between growth that feels heavy and growth that feels sustainable.

People: Are You Settling for Warm Bodies?

Finally, there is the most visible barrier, and often the most avoided.

Settling.

Not settling for mediocre intentions but settling for misalignment. Keeping people in roles where they are tolerated rather than fully trusted. Prioritizing loyalty over performance. Avoiding difficult conversations because replacing someone feels disruptive.

Dominic Monkhouse, the former managing director of Pier 1 and the leader who scaled Rackspace's UK division from zero to £30 million in five years asks one key question: "Would you enthusiastically rehire every member of your team?"[20] If not, something's off.

As businesses grow, the gap between average and exceptional widens. A single underperforming leader can create drag across the organization. High performers compensate. Energy shifts from innovation and getting shit done to containment and firefighting. Over time, the cost compounds.

Growth requires A-level performance in critical roles. Not because excellence is aspirational, but because complexity and growing a company demands it. When you're small, you want a 100 percent A-player team.

These four barriers—leadership capacity, market awareness, systems, and people—account for the majority of growth challenges I've seen in my years coaching CEOs and leadership teams. We'll explore each of them in much greater depth in the chapters ahead.

Before you dive into strategy, it's critical to understand what's truly holding you back. Only then can you set the right priorities for the coming quarter, and beyond.

20　Jean Moncrieff, "Episode 40: Dominic Monkhouse," *The Freedom Experience with Jean Moncrieff* (January, 2025).

FREEDOM FACTORS

1. GROWTH STALLS FOR PREDICTABLE REASONS

Leadership gaps, weak systems, market blindness, and settling for the wrong people are not random problems. They are structural constraints. If you name them clearly, you can address them deliberately.

2. LEADERSHIP IS ALMOST ALWAYS THE CONSTRAINT

If decisions bottleneck at you, if accountability is fuzzy, if standards are uneven, growth will eventually wobble. The business can only scale to the level of its leadership with you at the center.

3. FOUNDATIONS DETERMINE FREEDOM

You don't escape the weeds by pushing harder. You escape by strengthening the foundations beneath you so the business can carry its own weight.

CHAPTER 6:
Choosing a Clear Three-Year Destination

*"A three-year highly achievable goal is so human.
It's close enough that you can reach out and touch it—
and that's why it matters."*

—Shannon Byrne Susko

Before we tackle those growth barriers, let's step back and clarify where you want to be three years from now. By this point, I hope you have some sense of what may be holding you back.

Ideally, the previous chapters have prompted you to reflect on your purpose. Perhaps you've even jotted down thoughts about where you want to be ten years from now—the life you want to be living and the kind of business you want to be leading.

That long view matters. But let's be honest, ten years can feel like a lifetime, especially in the world we live in. It's inspiring, yes. But it's too distant to guide what you do on Monday morning.

Five years isn't much better. Beyond a certain point, forecasting turns into guessing.

Three years is different. As Shannon says, "It's close enough that you can reach out and touch it." Three years is just twelve quarters, and with focus, you can accomplish an extraordinary amount.

This chapter is about translating your long-term vision into a clear three-year goal. One that bridges your purpose and ten-year ambition with what needs to happen this quarter.

This isn't about creating a thick strategy document. It's about defining a first, clear marker for where you want to be three years from now. A simple, shared picture of what must be true if you're serious about building the business and the life you envision.

Why Three Years Matters

A long-term vision gives you direction, but it doesn't tell you what to do next. That's why the most effective leaders think in layered time horizons. They hold a ten-year vision as a compass—something that guides decisions and shape's identity—but they commit to a nearer destination that forces clarity.

In my experience, three years is the sweet spot. It's long enough to reshape a leadership team, tune your cash generation system, and build differentiators that competitors can't easily replicate. But it's short enough to feel tangible. You can imagine the milestones you'll need to achieve over the coming twelve quarters. You can map priorities to those milestones. And you can narrow your focus to achieving those goals and priorities.

Three years gives you enough runway to make meaningful change, but not so much that urgency disappears.

A Quick Word About Systems and Frameworks

Over the years, I've been exposed to most of the major business operating systems—the Entrepreneurial Operating System® (EOS), Scaling Up, The Great Game of Business,® and others. They all offer useful frameworks and tools, but there isn't one "right" system. Different businesses and teams require different structures at different stages of growth.

My own preference has gravitated toward a growth framework developed by Shannon Byrne Susko called Metronomics.® Full disclosure, I was a certified Metronomics coach before stepping into the CEO role at Small Giants.

What drew me to Metronomics is that it's less rigid and more of a growth framework. Susko and her global community of coaches—many of them former CEOs—are constantly scanning the landscape for ideas worth integrating into the framework.

At the center of the framework is something Susko calls a 3-Year Highly Achievable Goal,® (3HAG). And the 3HAG in Metronomics is the secret to connecting your long-term vision to your near-term reality.

Choosing a clear, specific three-year destination changes how a leadership team behaves. It forces you to say no to what isn't a priority (yes, even the shiny objects). It exposes wishful thinking. It clarifies what must be true—not just what would be nice. And it removes the wild-ass guessing that so often passes for long-term planning.

Throughout this section, I'll reference elements of Metronomics because it's the framework I know best. That's not a prescription. It's context. The deeper point isn't the system. It's the discipline.

A business operating system creates rhythm, clarity, and accountability. The right one is the one that fits where you are in your journey and supports the kind of company you're trying to build.

Whatever you choose, don't dabble. Commit to it. And if you can, work with a coach or implementer who knows the system deeply. Proper implementation makes all the difference between a framework that lives on paper and one that changes how your business runs.

Why One-Page Changes Everything

When a business is small, alignment is mostly easy. Everyone is close. Conversations happen in real time. Decisions are visible. You don't need a planning process because the plan lives in the room.

Then the business grows.

People move into different offices. New departments appear. Meetings multiply. Priorities stack up. And slowly, without anyone intending it, the business starts running on fragments—half-formed plans, old assumptions, and whatever feels most urgent this week.

I've experienced this firsthand—more than once. In the late nineties, when I co-founded a web content management company, we began aligned around a bold ambition: to build the world's first web content management system. There were seven of us working out of a loft, creating something that felt ahead of its time.

Our purpose was simple: democratize website content management. There was no WordPress back then. Our ten-year vision? To become what WordPress eventually became.

We talked about that vision constantly, not because we were especially disciplined, but because we had to be. Survival and sanity demanded alignment.

As Joel Trammell puts it in *The Chief Executive Operating System*, "At this stage, it's more about keeping your own sanity than keeping everyone on the same page."[21]

But as the business grew, the alignment and simplicity disappeared. We moved into bigger offices. We opened a London office. We hired more people. Communication started to fray. It wasn't that anyone stopped caring. It was that there was no longer a single, shared source of truth. Any planning we did lasted about as long as the time we took to create it.

Back then, frameworks like EOS, Scaling Up, and Metronomics weren't widely available. We didn't have a common language for alignment. We were all in our twenties without any business experience, flying by the seats of our pants.

One lesson did stick.

Ian Kilbride, an investor in our startup, encouraged us to hold a weekly meeting where everyone brought along their one-page plan. He used it to

---

21   John Trammell, Sam Sakr, *The Chief Executive Operating System: The Essential Playbook for Success in the CEO Role* (New York: P 180 Press, 2023).

structure discussion, focus attention, and keep the team aligned around what mattered most. Ian never made a big thing of it. He didn't sell it as a system. He simply insisted on the discipline, and it worked.

Before Ian introduced that rhythm, we were scattered. Instead of focusing on our number one goal, building the world's first open-source web content management platform, we chased shiny objects. We took on website development projects. We built a graphic design team. We even explored acquiring a design agency. It wasn't that these moves were wrong. It's that they weren't intentional, they were opportunistic and not part of a plan.

Looking back, a shared plan might have kept us more focused. It might even have helped us navigate the dot com crash of 2000. But the problems ran deeper. Our leadership team was wholly inexperienced and more than somewhat dysfunctional. The ideas were strong. We had a level of trust and commitment. But we lacked commitment, accountability, and attention to results. Our focus was fragmented. And we ultimately became another casualty of the dot com collapse.

Ian went on to do what he does best, building successful businesses and backing new ventures. I carried the lesson with me: as complexity grows, your leadership capability must grow and evolve. If it doesn't, the business stalls.

That is why a one-page plan matters. Not because it is fashionable. Because it forces clarity. For one, it narrows your focus and compels you to ask yourself a hard question: do I have the right people on the bus?

Secondly, when strategy is scattered across documents, buried in email threads, and locked in people's heads, everyone starts improvising. A one-page plan creates a shared point of reference. People stop guessing. Trade-offs become clearer. Priorities become visible.

A Three-Year Destination

We tend to treat planning as a one-time event—a retreat, a workshop, a few intense sessions around a table—after which the "real work" begins. But the strength of your plan doesn't lie in perfection, it exists in evolution. You must continuously evolve your plan as your understanding deepens and as the business grows.

That's why the starting point isn't building an elaborate, comprehensive strategy. It's gutting out where you want to be three years from now. Susko uses the term "Gut it Out"® deliberately. It captures the spirit of the exercise. You're not forecasting with precision or trying to predict every variable. You're taking what's currently in your head—the ambition, the assumptions, the goals—and putting it on paper.

From there, you begin asking practical questions. What do you want the business to look like thirty-six months from now? What must be true in twelve quarters for you to say you're on track? What metrics will tell you you're making real progress? What priorities need to rise to the top—and which ones need to fall away?

This first version will not be perfect. It shouldn't be. It is the starting point of a conversation with yourself and your leadership team. As the business evolves, the plan will evolve with it. And in that evolution, clarity compounds.

Susko's Gut it Out page looks something like the diagram on the next page. On the left are the elements that anchor you—purpose, core values, your ten-year goal and how you measure profit in your business. On the right is the three-year destination: the financial signals, the capabilities you must build, and a short statement that captures where you're heading.

Gut Out Your 3-Year Plan

Your 3-Year Goal

Year Ending:

Revenue:

Expenses:

Profit:

Cash in Bank:

Valuation:

Widgets:

3 Year Goal:

3-5 Key Capabilities

Known For:

Foundation 1

Core Purpose:

Core Values:

Foundation 2

10 Year Goal

Foundation 3

Profit/X

Adapted from the Metronomics 3HAG framework.

You are not building a complex plan. You are simply *gutting out* what's in your head on a single page. Broad strokes. Direction. A starting point.

Over time, that page will evolve to include. Quarterly and annual priorities. Metrics will become clearer. Capabilities will be refined. What begins as a rough draft will evolve into a disciplined process that guides your execution. But it can't evolve until it exists.

One of the most powerful aspects of doing this exercise is that it forces you to think about what your business looks like in three years' time. Specifically, what you are known for (value proposition) and the capabilities you need to build in order to create that competitive advantage.

In other words, you are breaking ground on your moat.

Shaping the Three-Year Horizon

The 3HAG page is intentionally simple. On the left are your foundations—core purpose, core values, your long-term goal, and the economic driver of the business.

Your foundations may not be perfect. They may not even fully existent. For now, simply capture what you have. In time, these will evolve.

On the right is the three-year horizon. This is where ambition becomes tangible. It's where you describe what must be true three years from now if you are serious about your purpose and long-term intent. Think of it as your first basecamp on the climb toward your long-term goal.

The goal is not perfection. It's clarity.

You are asking a small number of clear questions. What financial outcomes would signal meaningful progress? What level of profitability and cash strength would demonstrate resilience? How many "widgets" do we need to sell to hit our numbers? What's does the business look like in three years? What must it be capable of doing consistently and exceptionally well? What will it be known for three years from now?

When I took over the Small Giants Community, one of the first things I did with my team was run this exercise. I wanted to get my thinking out of my head and in front of them. But more than that, I wanted to lift the lid on their thinking and understand what they believed was possible.

CORE VALUES: THE GUARDRAILS FOR DECISION MAKING

We discussed ten-year thinking in the previous chapter. I explore purpose in more detail in the following chapter, but for now, think of purpose as the reason your business exists. In the next section, I'll walk through the importance of having an economic engine but first let's dive into Core Values.

Values shape decision-making. They inform culture. They determine who you hire, who you promote, and, when necessary, who you let go. When values are clear and consistently reinforced, they become the guardrails for leadership. They create alignment not through control, but through shared understanding.

For most companies, values hang on the wall, on a plaque by the front door, or on the company website. Sometimes leaders and employees can recall a few of them. Far fewer can point to a moment when those values shaped a difficult decision.

And that is the difference between a company that decorates its exterior with a list of values and a company truly driven by its values, where those values move from words on a website to forces that actively shape culture and decision making inside the organization.

Take Tasty Catering is a strong example. Their values include:

1. Always Moral, Ethical and Legal
2. Treat All with Respect
3. Quality in Everything We Do
4. High Customer Service Standards
5. A Competitive and Strong Determination to Be the Best
6. An Enduring Culture of Individual Discipline
7. Freedom and Responsibility within the Culture of Individual Discipline

Tasty has a longer list than I'd recommend. I'd suggest you keep your core values to between three and five, not a long list no one remembers—unless you're like Tasty. These folks know their values by number. They reference them in meetings. They use them to challenge decisions. They live them daily.

During the 2009 financial crisis,[22] when leadership initially considered layoffs, a senior leader pushed back, arguing that doing so would violate Value #1 and Value #2. Instead of reducing headcount, the company temporarily reduced working hours across the team. Jobs were preserved. Trust deepened. The culture strengthened under pressure.

That's what lived values look like. They guide decision making through the good *and* the tough times… especially during the tough times.

Like I said, your values don't need to be numerous. In fact, three to five is ideal. They should not be generic aspirations like "integrity" or "excellence"—those are table stakes. The real work is identifying the principles that are distinctive to your company, the ones that truly shape behavior.

---

22   Jean Moncrieff, "Episode 21: Tasty Catering's Cultural Revolution and Entrepreneurial Spirit with Tom Walter," *The Freedom Experience with Jean Moncrieff* (2024), https://www.jeanmoncrieff.com/podcasts/the-freedom-experience-with-jean-moncrieff/episodes/2148870579, accessed January 16, 2025.

In their *Culture Code*, Text-Em-All describe how, in October 2017, the entire company traveled to Austin, Texas for a facilitated retreat to uncover their core values. At the time, they already had a set of values, but they had not been created with input from the full team. That did not sit right.

During that retreat, they discovered, overwhelmingly, that Compassion, Authenticity, and Shared Excellence were their true core values. Simple. Memorable. Actionable.

I am not suggesting you need to fly your entire company to Austin to uncover your core values. Rather, values can evolve over time. Text-Em-All's founders defined their early values, and those values served them well in the beginning. But eventually, the time came to go deeper with the whole team and surface the values they truly shared.

Ask yourself the question: if you stopped someone in your organization and asked them to name your core values, could they? And would they be able to describe how those values influence daily decisions?

If the answer is no or even maybe, there is no better time than now to begin working on them with your team.

CLARIFYING YOUR ECONOMIC ENGINE

Part of shaping your three-year horizon involves getting clear on how your business makes money.

Collins described this as identifying the economic engine—the single denominator that most powerfully drives long-term profit, you're Profit per X.[23]

Collins proposed an essential question:

If you could pick one and only one ratio—profit per X—to systematically increase over time, what would X have the greatest and most sustainable impact on your economic engine?

---

23   Collins, *Good To Great.*

As an example, while most airlines were focused on maximizing profit per seat, Southwest Airlines identified their X as profit per plane. That focus shaped their strategic decisions around aircraft type, pricing model, routes, brand promises, and even their anti-brand promises, in other words, who they are not.

By tracking this, you make better, faster and *more strategic* decisions.

For one company, X might be profit per customer. For another, profit per employee. For a retailer, it could be profit per transaction. For a multi-location business, profit per location may be the most meaningful driver. The goal is not to invent a clever metric. It is to identify the core driver of value creation in your specific model.

Your foundations link to Collin's Hedge Hog Concept.

- What you are deeply passionate about? (your Core Purpose, or 'why'),

- What you can be the best at in the world? (your Core Competencies), and

- What best drives your economic engine? (your Profit per X)

When you identify the right X, strategy begins to sharpen. Investment decisions become clearer. Trade-offs become less emotional and more rational. You start to see which levers truly matter, and which ones are simply noise disguised as urgency.

More importantly, once you understand your economic engine, you can begin building your systems around it. Hiring decisions shift because you know the type of capability that improves the driver. Pricing discipline strengthens because you understand how margin interacts with scale. Operational processes begin aligning around improving that key denominator rather than chasing a collection of disconnected metrics.

Without this clarity, leadership teams often attempt to optimize everything at once—revenue, margin, headcount, customer acquisition, expansion— and end up diluting focus. With it, energy concentrates around what truly compounds value over time.

So, as you define your three-year horizon, ask yourself: What is the core driver of our economic engine? And how must it improve over the next three years to create sustainable strength?

BRIDGING THE GAP

On the left side of the page, your foundations anchor your long-term vision. You have clarity on why your business exists, the values that guide your decisions, and what fuels your growth.

On the right side, you articulate what must become true over the next three years if you are serious about your long-term vision.

It is about defining a clear, shared destination, the basecamp you are climbing toward. What financial outcomes would signal meaningful progress? What level of profitability and cash strength would confirm the business is healthy? What capabilities must you build to truly differentiate your business and perhaps become the best in the world at what you do?

This is where your three-year goal comes into focus. Whether you call it a 3HAG, three-year picture, or your three-year vision, the discipline is the same. You are choosing a goal that excites you and pulls your team closer to your long-term goal without overwhelming you.

On the right, agree on your revenue, expenses, profit, cash in the bank, and the number of widgets sold. A widget might be the number of cases of iced tea you need to sell to reach your revenue target, or the number of software subscribers required to hit your goal. Widgets make the numbers tangible. They give you a clear sense of what must be sold to achieve your revenue target.

Equally important is the short narrative that describes where you are heading. When written clearly, it enables anyone in the organization to articulate the destination without opening a spreadsheet. Your statement should be a simple one-liner: to be the most trusted leadership development platform in North America.

You will also identify a handful of key capabilities you must develop to differentiate your business and position it to become best in the world at what you do. And finally, define what you are known for in three years? For Small Giants we want to be known for: creating exceptional next-gen leaders.

ROLLING DESTINATIONS AND COMPOUNDING MOMENTUM

A three-year goal is not a one-time destination. It functions more like a basecamp than a finish line.

Climbers do not ascend Everest in a single push. They move in stages, establishing basecamps along the way. Each basecamp allows them to regroup, reassess, and prepare for the next ascent. Progress is deliberate, not reckless.

Your three-year destination works the same way. It is a near-term summit that moves you meaningfully closer to your long-term ambition. When one destination is reached, the next becomes visible.

This rhythm creates momentum without burnout. It replaces vague long-term dreaming with structured forward motion. And it prevents the organization from becoming paralyzed by the scale of its ultimate ambition.

The discipline is simple: long-term direction, near-term clarity, continuous refinement.

WHY THIS WORKS

What you are creating here is the early foundation of what will become a **One-Page Strategic Plan**. You are not attempting to engineer the entire structure at once. You are establishing the outline—the first articulation of direction that can be refined over time.

In later chapters, we will introduce execution rhythms, meeting cadence, and accountability systems that make this living document operational. But none of that works without a shared destination.

Most businesses struggle not because they lack ambition, but because ambition is fragmented. Leaders describe different futures. Teams pursue disconnected priorities. Energy disperses. A clearly articulated three-year destination concentrates that energy. It gives the leadership team a shared reference point. It creates confidence. And confidence changes how people show up.

CASE STUDY: SHANNON SUSKO—FROM DESPERATE CEO TO LIFE-ALTERING EXITS

When Susko was leading Paradata, the company looked like a success story.

They had raised more than $30 million in funding. Revenue was growing at over 30 percent year over year. The market opportunity was real. From the outside, it appeared the business was doing exactly what high-growth venture-backed companies are supposed to do.

Inside, it felt very different.

The team was stretched. Systems weren't fully connected. Despite strong top-line growth, profitability and cash discipline were not where they needed to be. Susko found herself doing strategic thinking late at night after long days of firefighting. The company was moving fast, but it wasn't aligned. There was effort everywhere, yet very little traction.

Growth had outpaced structure.

The turning point did not begin with a perfect strategy document. It began with something far simpler—and far more uncomfortable.

Susko and her leadership team committed to defining a clear three-year destination. Not a vague aspiration. Not a five-year fantasy. A specific, measurable three-year target—what she later formalized as a 3HAG.

She describes the power of three years as "so human."[24] It's close enough to reach out and touch. Five years can feel abstract. Ten years feels distant. But three years creates tension. It forces a team to declare a score they are willing to be held accountable to.

When they first set it, the team walked out of the room thinking, *This could be so wrong*. But something shifted the moment it was declared. As Shannon puts it, A-players don't like to lose. Once the score was clear, the conversation immediately moved from *if* to *how*.

They didn't start with a polished **One-Page Strategic Plan**. They started by getting their thinking onto a single page—purpose, values, long-term ambition, revenue, expenses, profit, cash, and the key levers that would drive performance. It was rough. It was imperfect. But it was visible.

And that visibility changed behavior.

When Susko presented the simplified page to her board, she worried it might look too basic. Instead, the reaction surprised her. The clarity calmed them.

24	Jean Moncrieff, "Episode 23: From Desperate CEO to Life-Changing Exits: Shannon Byrne Susko's Journey," *The Freedom Experience with Jean Moncrieff* (2024), https://youtu.be/0eXa3PN6-w0?si=0zL3n3BtUyaknlk9, accessed December 13, 2024.

She showed where they were going. She showed the key drivers. She showed what it would look like when they arrived. The simplicity created confidence.

That first version did not stay static. Over time, the rough draft evolved into a disciplined **One-Page Strategic Plan** supported by execution rhythms and a stronger financial system. They began forecasting their key drivers—what Susko calls "widgets"—and, critically, forecasting cash. The breakthrough wasn't just setting a three-year goal. It was building behavioral discipline around the economic engine of the business.

Alignment began to compound. Decisions became clearer. Trade-offs became less emotional. The team stopped reacting to urgency and started executing against a shared destination.

Within six years, Susko led two successful exits. The experience became the foundation for what later evolved into the Metronomics Business Growth System.

FREEDOM FACTORS

1. CLARIFY YOUR GUARDRAILS

Purpose explains why you exist. Core values guide how you behave. If your values aren't shaping hiring, firing, and hard decisions, they aren't real yet. Make them clear, memorable, and lived.

2. IDENTIFY YOUR ECONOMIC ENGINE

Determine the one key driver—your Profit per X—that has the greatest long-term impact on your business model. Build your systems, pricing, hiring, and priorities around strengthening that driver.

3. CHOOSE A CLEAR THREE-YEAR DESTINATION

Stop trying to perfect a long-range master plan. Define what must be true in thirty-six months if you are serious about your purpose (financially, strategically, and operationally) and refine it as you go.

CHAPTER 7:
Building a High-Performing Leadership Team

*"One of the first things I did was sit the team down and say,
'I'm not sure what to do—and I need your help.'"*

—Elizabeth Glasbrenner

Once you've gutted out your three-year picture, one thing should become obvious: you cannot get there alone.

Purpose gives direction. A three-year goal creates alignment. But leadership is what turns both into reality.

In the early years of a business, the founder is the engine. You make the decisions, solve the problems, close the deals, calm the customers, and carry the weight. That intensity fuels early success. It creates speed. It creates focus. It creates momentum.

But it does not scale.

The very model that got you here will eventually hold you back. The informal, founder driven system that once created agility begins to fracture under the weight of complexity. As revenue grows, teams expand. New products are added. Markets widen. What once lived in your head now needs to live in the organization.

If it does not, you become the bottleneck.

Growth stalls. Decisions slow. Alignment drifts. Not because you lack capability, but because no single human can indefinitely carry the cognitive, emotional, and strategic load of a scaling business.

The shift from founder centric to team led is one of the hardest transitions an owner will ever make. It is also one of the most liberating.

This chapter is about making that shift deliberately.

When the Game Changes

Dominic Monkhouse offers an analogy that captures this shift clearly. He compares start-ups and scale-ups to two different sports.

In basketball, a team can win on the strength of a couple of star players. The game is influenced disproportionately by the strongest performers. Malcolm Gladwell refers to this as a strong-link system. Excellence at the top can compensate for weakness elsewhere.

That is how most early-stage businesses operate. The founder is the star player. A handful of talented individuals carry the rest. Speed and brilliance compensate for gaps.

But as a company grows, the game changes.

Scale-ups resemble football. In football, success does not depend on one superstar. It depends on the collective performance of the entire team. A single weak link can undermine the effort of everyone else. Coordination, positioning, and trust matter as much as talent.

As your business scales, you are no longer playing basketball. You are playing football. The system becomes weak-link driven. The lowest level of leadership capability on your team begins to determine your ceiling.

This is why A-players are not optional. They are essential.

The A-Player Leadership Team

One of your top priorities as a CEO is to build a high-performing leadership team. Everything else rests on this foundation.

Now, you might say to me, "But Jean, I already have a leadership team."

To which my response would be, "Do you? Are the people who got you here the people to lead you toward your three-year goal? Or are some of them holding you back?"

The mistake most business owners make is to define A-players by performance alone. Targets hit. Projects delivered. Revenue generated. Results matter, but they are not enough.

A true A-player performs in alignment with your values. And this is why it's so important to capture your core values and start living by them. Because performance without values alignment creates cultural debt. The numbers may look strong in the short term but trust quietly erodes underneath. Over time, that erosion weakens team cohesion and caps growth. Team members become more concerned with their own fiefdoms than the shared purpose of the business.

When evaluating leaders, I encourage owners to look through two lenses. First, values alignment. Does this person consistently live out the company's core values? Do their decisions reflect them? Do they strengthen the culture around them?

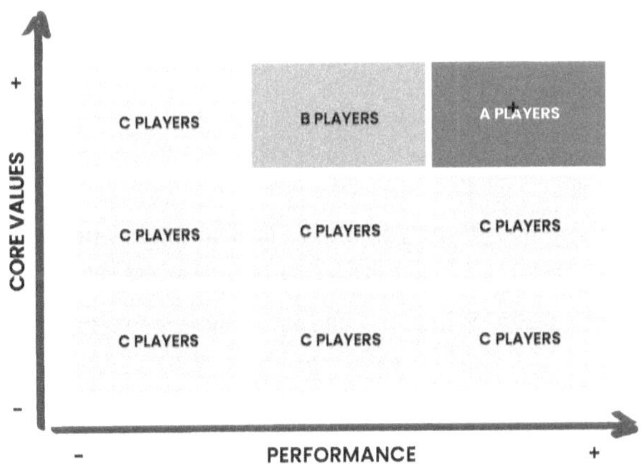

Second, performance excellence. Do they meet or exceed expectations? Do they take ownership? Do they deliver measurable outcomes?

- Your A-players sit in the upper right quadrant.
- B-players meet expectations and, with coaching, will exceed expectations
- All the rest are C-players

These two dimensions are not equal. Values come first. Skills can be developed. Values rarely can. The mistake most business owners make is holding onto C-players for too long, especially on the leadership team.

A simple way to test your leadership team is to ask yourself two questions.

1. If this person received an external offer tomorrow, would I fight to keep them?
2. Would I enthusiastically rehire them today?

If the answer to either question is no, treat it as a signal. As you scale, even one weak link on the leadership team can quietly cap your growth.

From Founder Centric to Team Led

There are two excuses I hear for not hiring A-players: "I can't afford to hire A–players" and "I can't find any A-players." The truth is you can't afford not to find and recruit A-players. And there is a way to do this without breaking the bank.

Go one role at a time.

Sit down and list everything you do in a typical week. The hats you wear. Every meeting. Every decision. Every fire you put out. Then ask yourself: what gives me energy? What am I bad at? What consistently drains me?

Chances are that a significant portion of your week is spent doing work you are no longer the best person to be doing. Work that sits in your competence zone, not your genius zone. Work that if you found the right person would accelerate your growth.

Start with a single role. If you could hire only one A-player, which seat would you fill first?

When I first did this exercise, the gap was obvious. It was finance.

I had a bookkeeper, but I was still carrying the real accountability for the function. It was one of the many hats I wore. Then our accountants came to me with a $700,000 tax bill. That was the moment I knew I needed help.

So, I hired Kevin, a fractional chief financial officer.

Kevin wasn't cheap. But he helped me navigate the tax issue, installed systems and discipline in our finance function, and lifted a significant weight off my shoulders. That single A-Player hire freed me to focus on the parts of the business where I added the most value.

Figure out where you most need an A-player. Then go out and find someone who loves that role and is exceptionally good at it. Someone who aligns with your values and mission. Someone who brings depth and expertise you simply do not have. The right person will often pay for themselves within the first ninety days.

Then repeat the process.

I agree, finding A-players isn't easy. That's why it's so important to have clarity on your purpose, your values, and your goals. A-players want to be part of a winning team. They want to make a dent in the universe, and they're attracted to companies on a mission. It's not enough to have a purpose. You need to get out there and tell the world about it. And you need to constantly be on the lookout for A-players. They might be the server at your local café or the salesperson who sold you your car. You have to tune in your A-player radar.

Transitioning from a founder-led growth model to an A-player leadership team doesn't happen overnight. It may take three or four quarters, some-times longer. But the sooner you stop trying to be the smartest person in the room and start building a team of A-players, the sooner your business will gain traction.

Super Whos

Dr. Benjamin Hardy introduces a powerful concept in *The Science of Scaling: The Super Who*.[25]

While an A-player exceeds expectations, a Super Who knows the exact path to get you where you need to go, and fast. They have seen the terrain before. They have navigated complexity at scale. They understand the hidden traps and the blind spots.

If your three-year goal is to grow your business tenfold, then finding Super Whos is non-negotiable. They are force multipliers. They shorten your learning curve, reduce costly experimentation, and bring the kind of pattern recognition that accelerates execution.

Like A-players, finding Super Whos is not easy. The same rules apply: you have to put in the work to attract and excite them to your cause and you have to constantly be on the lookout for them.

Structure Before Titles

Even strong leaders struggle without clarity.

Many businesses operate with impressive titles and vague accountability. People sit around the table with authority in theory but ambiguity in practice.

Instead of starting with titles, start with functions. Every business relies on a handful of core functions such as sales, marketing, operations, finance, and people. The labels matter less than the clarity of ownership.

Each function must have clear decision-making authority, defined outcomes and metrics, and one accountable leader.

When accountability is fuzzy, you (the business owner) remain the default decision-making system. When ownership is clear, leaders can act with confidence and speed.

---

25   Hardy and Erickson, *The Science of Scaling*.

Structure does not replace leadership. It enables it.

But even with strong A-players and clear accountability, one final ingredient determines whether a leadership team truly performs.

Cohesion.

Building True Cohesion

Patrick Lencioni's work reminds us that teams rarely fail because of a lack of talent. They fail because of breakdowns in trust, conflict, commitment, accountability, and focus on results.

I have worked with leadership teams at every stage of growth, and cohesion is one of the greatest challenges to building a high-performing leadership team. Let me put it simply: when you sit down around the table, there must be a high level of trust amongst everyone around the table. Everyone around the table must feel like they matter and that they can be vulnerable, including you. You want to encourage heated debates, but make sure everyone walks away aligned around a common goal—what's best for the business.

It takes time to build a cohesive team, which is why hiring to values matters so much. Shared values and a shared goal are the foundation. You can't afford to have individuals focused only on their own function. Cohesion requires people to think beyond their lane and commit to the success of the whole.

We'll explore cohesion in more depth in the coming chapters, but for now, let me share a simple technique I use to test how cohesive a team really is.

One of the most effective disciplines I use is the **30-Day Huddle Challenge**. A daily, fifteen-minute standing meeting with a fixed agenda: good news, the top priority for the day, and where you are stuck.

On the surface, it seems too simple to matter. In reality, it reveals resistance.

The individuals who push back on the **Huddle** often say they're too busy for another meeting or that they don't see the value. What it signals to me is the people who aren't truly committed to the shared goal, those who prefer to operate alone and resist visibility and accountability, they're not playing for the team. And unless that changes quickly, they shouldn't be on it.

CASE STUDY: ELIZABETH GLASBRENNER AND THE COURAGE TO CHOOSE PEOPLE OVER CONTROL

Glasbrenner did not step into the CEO role at Smiley Technologies after years of careful succession planning. Her brother left the family business abruptly. One day he was there. The next, he was not. Glasbrenner found herself at the helm without a long runway or a clean handover.

Her brother had been exactly the leader the company needed in its early years. He was gritty, technical, and deeply involved in every decision. That leadership style had taken the company from zero to roughly 3 to 4 million in revenue. It worked until the business required something different.

Glasbrenner did not respond by trying to replicate her brother's style. Instead, she gathered the team and said, "I'm not sure what to do, and I need your help." That act of vulnerability set a different tone.

But one senior technical leader began to undermine her quietly. He positioned himself as indispensable, controlled information, and resisted shared accountability. Glasbrenner tolerated it longer than she should have because she feared losing critical expertise.

Eventually, she made the decision to let him go.

The consequences were immediate. Nearly 30 percent of the company walked out in the weeks that followed. Every Friday brought another resignation. It would have been easy to retreat into control.

Instead, Glasbrenner drew a clear line. She gathered the remaining team, rented a bus, and told them plainly that if they were committed to the future of the business, they would get on. Only one person did not.

That moment reset the company. It clarified belonging, accountability, and shared leadership.

Under Glasbrenner's leadership, Smiley Technologies broke through its plateau and grew beyond nineteen million in revenue while remaining profitable and debt-free. The transformation did not come from heroics. It came from building a leadership team aligned around values and shared accountability.

Her story is a reminder that leadership is not about control. It is about courage, clarity, and trust.

FREEDOM FACTORS

1. STOP BEING THE HERO

The leadership style that got you here will not get you there. If your business still depends on you to make every critical decision, you are the bottleneck. Your job is no longer to be the strongest link. It is to build a team where no position is weak—and where leadership is shared, not centralized.

2. CHOOSE LEADERS WHO EMBODY YOUR VALUES

Performance without values alignment is a short-term gain and a long-term liability. True A-players deliver results *and* strengthen culture. If you wouldn't fight to keep them—or enthusiastically rehire them—you already have your answer. Leadership quality is a strategic decision, not a sentimental one.

3. DESIGN ACCOUNTABILITY, THEN BUILD COHESION

Clarity precedes trust. Every core function must have single-point accountability, clear outcomes, and decision authority. Once structure is clear, cohesion becomes possible. Daily rhythm, visibility, and psychological safety turn a group of capable individuals into a leadership team that can scale without you.

CHAPTER 8:
Your Execution Engine

*"Most of us don't have strategy issues,
we have an inability to deliver what we've promised."*

—Patrick Thean

I can remember taking my leadership team off-site on numerous occasions. One year we booked out a hotel and locked ourselves away for two days of strategy. Another time we headed to a game farm and spent several days together mapping out what the future could look like. Those sessions were energizing. We debated, we challenged one another, and we painted a compelling picture of what we wanted to achieve in the year ahead.

At one point, we even tied a goal to the Summer Olympics. The ambition was specific: grow the business to a certain size so that by the time the Games arrived, we could moor our yacht off the coastline of Athens and be there to experience it. It was vivid, motivating, and shared. Sitting in that strategy session, it felt entirely achievable.

The difficulty was never in setting the direction. It was in what happened afterward. When we returned to the office, the gravitational pull of the day-to-day took over. Customer issues resurfaced, operational demands intensified, and new opportunities distracted us. Instead of executing against a small number of clearly defined priorities, we slipped back into running the business reactively.

We were not short on effort. We were short on determination. Rather than protecting two or three critical priorities and aligning the organization around them, we allowed too many initiatives to compete for attention.

Our metrics were not consistently visible. Our meetings lacked a rhythm that forced accountability.

Before we knew it, another year had passed and were busier but no closer to our goal. The cycle would begin again: renewed ambition, another strategy conversation, another set of intentions. The pattern was not a failure of vision. It was a failure of execution.

Strategy without disciplined follow-through is little more than optimism. If the three-year destination defines where you are going, your execution engine determines whether you actually arrive.

In my experience, execution confidence rests on three pillars: clear priorities, meaningful metrics, and a consistent meeting rhythm. When these three elements work together, momentum builds. When they are absent, even the strongest strategy slowly unravels.

This chapter is about building that engine.

The Discipline of Execution

In my interview with Patrick Thean,[26] he made a point that has stayed with me: execution is often the single biggest differentiator between companies that scale and those that stall. Strategy is rarely the problem. Follow-through is.

The difference becomes obvious when you work closely with leadership teams. Some teams make commitments and treat them as non-negotiable. They adapt when needed, but they do not drift. Others speak enthusiastically about transformation yet struggle to translate intention into action. The gap is rarely intelligence. It is discipline. And honestly for around every ten companies I encounter, one team is playing the game to win.

---

26   Jean Moncrieff, "Episode 38: The Unexpected CEO Superpower: Curiosity Over Experience with Patrick Thean," *The Freedom Experience with Jean Moncrieff* (2025), https://www.jeanmoncrieff.com/podcasts/the-freedom-experience-with-jean-moncrieff/episodes/2148959992, accessed March 30, 2025.

Imagine the opportunity in that alone. Most of your competitors aren't willing to do the work. They've hardly crossed the start line when they drop out of the marathon.

It was only after we hired a coach and implemented systems like EOS and Great Game of Business® (GGOB) that we began to find traction. I suspect without a coach, we'd have given up before we had started. And it made a huge difference to how we operated.

Before that shift, our leadership meetings were chaotic. Conversations drifted into the crisis of the moment. Critical issues were postponed. Priorities were ignored. We left the room having talked well past the allotted time and decided very little. More often than not, we scheduled a follow up meeting just to spend more time circling the same issue.

Bringing a coach into the mix forced us to adopt a more structured meeting cadence. Instead of letting the loudest issue dictate the agenda, the meeting itself began to drive the direction. We moved from highly unproductive sessions to a focused and consistent rhythm. Priorities were clarified. Numbers were reviewed regularly. Accountability became visible. Meetings became shorter and more decisive. And soon momentum improved because we worked on the right things.

Execution does not require complexity. It requires consistency.

PILLAR ONE: CLEAR PRIORITIES

When Steve Jobs returned to Apple in 1997, he encountered a company overwhelmed by its own product complexity. Rather than layering on more initiatives, he reduced the entire product line to four core categories. That act of ruthless prioritization laid the foundation for one of the most remarkable turnarounds in business history.

The principle is simple but difficult: progress accelerates when focus narrows.

In my own business, I did the opposite for years. I chased opportunities, convinced that revenue growth alone would fix structural issues. Each January, we would define a strategy. By February, I would pivot toward a new idea that felt more exciting. The entrepreneurial instinct that helped us spot opportunity also made us susceptible to distraction.

Execution improved only when I accepted that discipline meant saying no. We limited ourselves to a small number of quarterly priorities and refused to add new ones midstream. We committed to finishing what we started.

Priorities must cascade. Your daily actions should clearly connect to your longer-term ambition:

- Long-term vision (BHAG)
- Three-year destination
- Annual goals
- Quarterly priorities
- Weekly focus

When that cascade is intact, effort compounds. When it breaks, teams become busy but unfocused. Revenue may increase while margins erode. New opportunities pull attention away from core commitments. Activity replaces progress.

Strong execution comes from choosing less, not more. Limiting priorities to three to five at each level forces clarity. Every initiative should visibly support the level above it. Anything that does not should be questioned.

PILLAR TWO: MEANINGFUL METRICS

Priorities without metrics are aspirations.

Imagine watching a football match without a scoreboard. The players might run hard, the crowd might cheer, but no one would know whether progress is being made. Many organizations operate exactly this way.

At Tasty Catering, performance is made visible in a simple but powerful way. Each week, the company gathers for lunch. A scoreboard sits at the front of the room. As numbers are called out, the accountable leader shares the result. Someone climbs a ladder and writes the figures in real time. Revenue, cost of sales, profit. Nothing hidden.

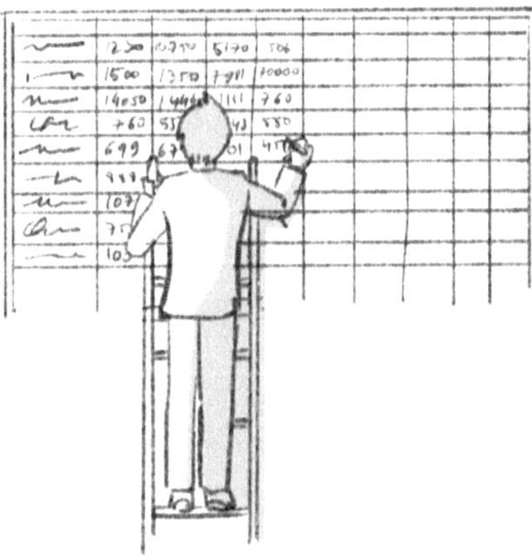

That visibility changes behavior. Numbers stop being abstract. They become shared commitments.

The lesson is not about ladders or lunchrooms. It is about transparency. Metrics should provide real-time feedback, enable course correction, and create clarity about ownership. When people understand the numbers and see them regularly, they begin thinking differently. They start acting like stewards rather than employees.

Jack Stack's work on Open Book Management[27] reinforces this principle. When teams understand how the business makes money, and how their actions influence results, engagement increases. Metrics are not tools of control. They are tools of alignment.

Choose a small number of leading indicators tied directly to your priorities. Review them consistently. Make them visible. The discipline of measurement strengthens the discipline of execution.

---

27   Jack Stack, Bo Burlingham, *The Great Game of Business: The Only Sensible Way to Run a Business* (New York: Crown Currency, 2013).

PILLAR THREE: CONSISTENT MEETING RHYTHM

Execution does not sustain itself. It requires rhythm.

Structured meetings create alignment and prevent drift. Without them, misalignment quietly grows. Assumptions go unchallenged. Commitments fade. Urgent issues crowd out important ones.

A disciplined cadence typically includes:

- A short daily huddle focused on metrics and immediate priorities
- A weekly tactical meeting to review progress and remove obstacles
- A monthly or quarterly session to confirm strategic alignment

The purpose of these meetings is not conversation for its own sake. It is decision making and accountability. Good news is shared. Numbers are reviewed. Stuck points are surfaced. Ownership is clarified.

When meetings are structured well, they reduce confusion rather than create it. They shorten decision cycles. They reinforce clarity. Most importantly, they prevent the organization from drifting back into reactive mode.

The cost of this rhythm is small, relative to its impact. Even a structured cadence consumes only a small percentage of available working time. The return on clarity and momentum far outweighs the time invested.

Execution thrives on rhythm.

Type	Purpose	Who	Frequency
Daily Huddle	Share good news, metrics, priorities	Leadership Team	Daily: 15 min or less
Weekly Tactical	Review and plan priorities	Leadership Team	Weekly: 1 hrs or less
Monthly Strategy	Confirmation / 90-day execution review	Leadership Team	Monthly: 4 hrs or less
Monthly Townhall	Align the entire company	Entire Company	1 hr or less

Type	Purpose	Who	Frequency
Quarterly Strategy	Confirmation / 90-day execution review	Leadership Team	1 day
Annual Strategy	Deep dive offsite	Leadership Team	2 days

Metronomics Execution Cadence[28]

Finding the Right Execution System

Different businesses require different tools at different stages. Some leaders resonate with EOS. Others engage deeply with The Great Game of Business. Others integrate strategy and execution through frameworks like Metronomics.

The system matters less than the commitment to it.

The danger lies not in choosing the wrong framework, but in half-implementing the right one. Execution requires discipline. If you adopt a system, commit to it fully. Work with someone who understands it deeply. Allow it to shape behavior rather than sit in a binder.

The goal is not to collect frameworks. It is to build consistency.

Bringing It Together

Strategy defines direction. Leadership provides capability. Execution creates movement.

Without an execution engine, your three-year destination remains a concept. With one, it becomes achievable. Clear priorities focus effort. Meaningful metrics provide feedback. A consistent rhythm sustains momentum.

This is how ambition turns into results.

---

28   Shannon Byrne Susko, *Metronomics: One United System to Grow Up Your Team, Company, and Life* (Seattle: Lioncrest Publishing, 2021).

FREEDOM FACTORS

1. RUTHLESSLY LIMIT PRIORITIES

Define no more than three to five quarterly priorities that directly support your three-year destination. Protect them. Evolve them. Finish them. Say no to distractions that dilute focus.

2. MAKE THE SCORE VISIBLE

Identify the few metrics that truly matter and review them weekly. Ensure ownership is clear and performance is transparent. What gets measured consistently gets improved.

3. INSTALL A DISCIPLINED RHYTHM

Commit to a structured cadence of daily, weekly, and quarterly meetings. Use them to review priorities, address obstacles, and reinforce account-ability. Execution is sustained through rhythm, not motivation.

CHAPTER 9:
Mastering Your Cash System

"The key to making money in your business lies in the widgets—the non-financial things that flow through your organization."

—Shannon Susko

Revenue is seductive. It looks impressive on paper. It energizes a sales team. It gives you something to celebrate. But revenue alone doesn't make a business strong.

Profit matters more. It tells you whether your model works. It tells you whether your pricing, delivery, and cost structure are aligned. But even profit can mislead. A business can show accounting profit and still run out of cash.

Cash is what ultimately determines your freedom. Cash pays salaries. Cash funds growth. Cash gives you options. Cash lets you sleep at night.

Most small and mid-sized businesses ride a cash-flow rollercoaster. There are months, quarters, even years when everything feels abundant. Deals land. Payments clear. The bank balance looks healthy. Growth seems to come naturally.

Then something happens. The market shifts and your product or service becomes less relevant. A large account runs into trouble and affects your cashflow. A key project overruns. Key clients start shifting to an alternative product or supplier. Suddenly, the pressure builds.

That sudden change of pressure can trigger owners to drift toward the Doom Loops we discussed in chapter 2.

When cash tightens, we react. We push the sales team harder. We slash marketing spend. We delay investments. We chase opportunities outside our niche. We convince ourselves that a new product or service will change our trajectory. Sometimes it does. But the underlying problem remains unchanged.

What we rarely do is step back and ask: why does this keep happening? How can we create a more reliable cash engine.

Turns out, the deeper problem is that most business owners don't look at cash generation holistically. We zoom in on one part of the machine at a time. When revenue dips, our attention shifts to sales and marketing. When customers complain, we focus on operations. When the bank balance is tight, we're chasing payments.

Each move feels logical in isolation. But cash is not created in isolation. Before long, you're reacting to symptoms and playing a game of whack-a-mole instead of fixing the system.

Your Cash Engine

A reliable cash system is not the result of one strong function. It is the result of key functions working together, in sequence, with clarity and accountability. When those functions operate in silos instead of in unison, the system begins to splutter.

I once worked with a company that had built what appeared to be a powerful growth engine. Sales and marketing were firing on all cylinders. The company had just pushed past $20 million in revenue and were targeting $25 million within the year.

On the surface, everything looked healthy.

But sales was closing deals faster than operations could deliver. Projects slipped. Implementation timelines stretched. Customers grew frustrated. Quality began to wobble. Eventually cancellations increased, reputation suffered, and growth reversed. Instead of reaching $25 million, the business slid back toward $15 million.

The issue was not their ability to sell. The sales team was outperforming expectations. The problem was that the key business functions were not working in unison. They were operating in silos, with limited cohesion at the leadership level.

Cash flow problems are rarely just sales problems. They are usually organization-wide problems.

Think of your business like a high-performance engine. Marketing is the fuel intake. Sales compresses and ignites that fuel. Operations transfers power to the wheels by delivering value. Finance converts motion into cash in the bank. If one part misfires, overheats, or runs out of capacity, the whole engine loses power. You may still be moving, but you are burning fuel inefficiently and risking long-term damage.

Underpricing erodes margin. Over-hiring drains working capital. Poor invoicing slows payment. Weak forecasting creates structural strain between demand and capacity. None of these show up immediately in revenue, but all of them affect cash flow (*and profit*).

When you zoom out, it becomes clear: cash is not a finance department issue. It is a leadership *team* issue.

Your cash system is about how value is created, delivered, captured, and converted into cash in the bank. It is about whether your leadership team understands the economic engine of the business and manages the flow deliberately.

One way to think about this is what are the "widgets"—the non-financial units—that flow through your organization to land cash in the bank: leads to appointments, appointment to proposals, proposals to sales, sales to onboarding, onboarding to invoicing, and invoicing to cash in the bank. Cash is the outcome of widgets being handed from one function to another and those functions working in unison.

If you can visualize that system, you can strengthen it.

If you strengthen it, you reduce volatility.

If you reduce volatility, you increase freedom.

Mastering your cash system is about designing a business where value flows smoothly, margin is protected, and cash conversion becomes predictable rather than reactive.

Cash Can Set You Free

One practical way to make this visible is through a Key Function Flow Map (KFFM), developed by Shannon Byrne Susko in *The 3HAG Way*.[29] The principle is simple: Cash is generated by the flow of widgets (non-financial units) through your business. Leads become proposals. Proposals become orders. Orders become delivered work. Delivered work becomes invoices. Invoices become cash.

Sounds simple, right? You're probably thinking that you do this already. But I'll bet you're doing it in a siloed view. You're not looking at the big picture and the relationships between each of the functions involved.

The KFFM lays that flow out clearly. It shows how demand is created, how value is delivered, and where breakdowns silently restrict cash long before the impact appears in your bank account. More importantly, it forces accountability across the leadership team. Each function owns its part of the flow, and everyone can see how upstream delays affect downstream results.

When leaders understand how their decisions influence the entire system, conversations shift. Issues are surfaced earlier. Forecasts become more accurate. Bottlenecks are addressed before they become crises. Instead of reacting to cash shortages, the team begins managing the health of the system itself.

When the system works, cash becomes more predictable. And predictability reduces pressure. It creates space to think strategically instead of

---

29   Shannon Byrne Susko, *3HAG Way: The Strategic Execution System that ensures your strategy is not a Wild-Ass-Guess!* (Shannon Susko, 2018).

tactically. It allows you to lead instead of firefight. It restores the sense that the business is serving you, rather than the other way around. And most importantly, it improves your profitability.

That is what mastering your cash system really means.

Building Your Cash Generation System

Let's go back to Susko's KFFM. The idea is simple, yet powerful: map the flow of widgets through your business so your leadership team can visualize the process of evolving widgets into cash in the bank.

Think of it like a relay race. Marketing hands qualified opportunities (widget 1) to sales. Sales converts those opportunities into committed customers (widget 2). Operations delivers the product or service (widget 3) profitably. Finance invoices and collects cash in under thirty days (widget 4). Each team runs its leg of the race. The handoff matters as much as the individual performance.

When you map that flow, the conversation changes. Cash stops being a sales or finance problem and becomes a leadership responsibility.

To start building your own cash map, gather your leadership team and answer four questions:

1. What are the three to five core functions that directly generate cash?

2.   What are the key non-financial signals that move between those functions? (For example: qualified leads, signed contracts, projects delivered, invoices issued.)

3.   Who is clearly accountable for each function?

4.   What simple metrics tell you whether each stage is healthy and profitable?

The trick is not to overcomplicate your picture. Stick to three to five core functions. Sure, you have other functions like development or human resources, but they're supporting functions. They're not directly involved in the process of landing cash in the bank.

When your map is visible, bottlenecks and issues are easier to spot. You can anticipate when sales are about to outrun delivery. You can see when marketing isn't performing optimally and forecast a sales dip. You can catch when invoicing discipline is slowing cash conversion.

And you can fix the right problem.

Your Leadership Team's Role

At the center of this system is your leadership team. Their job is not just to optimize their own department. It is to protect the flow of value and profit across the whole business. To rally together and solve problems as a team, before they hit.

Cash is not created in silos. It is created when leaders understand how their decisions affect the next stage in the flow. If marketing runs a promotion, sales and operations must be prepared to handle the extra volume. If customer onboarding is stretched, customers might leave negative reviews. If finance tolerates loose payment terms, working capital tightens.

Strong leadership teams review this flow together weekly. They forecast together. They agree on realistic capacity. They align pricing with delivery capability. They protect margin deliberately rather than assuming profit will "show up" at the end.

When this alignment exists, cash becomes more predictable. When it does not, the business feels volatile even when revenue is rising.

Monitoring the Health of the System

The KFFM is a working map that shows how key functions connect, how widgets move between them, and where breakdowns quietly slow cash before anyone notices the impact on the bank account.

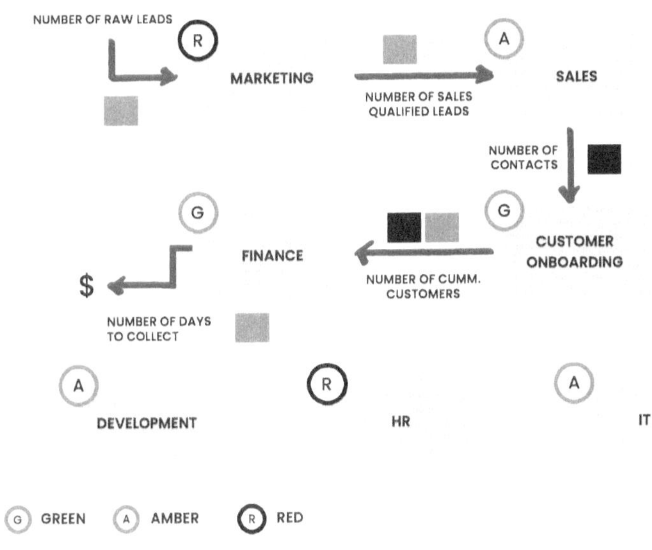

Adapted from Shannon Byrne Susko, Metronomics

Each function in your cash engine should have at least one leading indicator that signals whether the system is healthy. For example, if the number of Sales Qualified Leads drops, it may point to a seasonal fluctuation—or it may signal a deeper issue in how marketing is attracting and qualifying demand.

In the example diagram, marketing is showing red, sales is amber, and customer onboarding is green. When the leadership team reviews the map together, their instinct will be to focus on marketing and sales. That makes sense. But there is a second-order effect to consider. If marketing and sales are fixed aggressively without adjusting capacity, customer onboarding could quickly shift from green to red. One constraint simply moves downstream.

This is why these indicators are not just performance metrics. They are signals of overall function health. A team may technically be "hitting the numbers" and still be red. Marketing might be achieving its targets while the team is overstretched, lead quality is deteriorating, or the cost of acquisition is quietly eroding margin. The metric looks fine. The function is not.

The goal is to look beyond isolated numbers and assess health in the context of your entire cash generation engine.

You do not need a complex dashboard to do this. A simple red-amber-green view is often enough. If lead quality drops, that is an early warning. If delivery capacity tightens, that is an early warning. If margin begins to slip on projects, that is an early warning. These signals appear long before cash actually tightens.

Review them weekly. Re-forecast them quarterly. Treat red and amber signals as quarterly leadership priorities.

The power of this approach is not in the colors or the diagram. It is in the conversations it forces. When leaders can see the flow clearly, they stop defending their lane and start strengthening the system.

Keep Tuning Your Engine

A cash system rarely fails because it is too complicated. It fails because the leadership rhythm breaks down.

- Quarterly, align targets to your cash and profit goals
- Monthly, review capacity and margin assumptions
- Weekly, track leading indicators
- Daily, surface blockers early

Over time, this rhythm embeds discipline. It reduces volatility. And it lays the groundwork for a reliable cash generation system.

CASE STUDY: CATHERINE DAHL AND TURNING CASH FLOW INTO A SYSTEM AT BEANWORKS

When Dahl stepped into the CEO role at Beanworks, she wasn't taking over a polished, high-growth SaaS company.

The business had already been through a near-collapse. The original company had failed, investors had been burned, and the product itself needed to be rebuilt from the ground up. Dahl restarted Beanworks with a small, committed team, a handful of customers, and recurring revenue measured in the hundreds of thousands—not millions.

What she did have was clarity about one thing: if the company was going to survive and scale, it couldn't rely on heroics or intuition. It needed a system.

As the business began to grow, Dahl and her leadership team implemented the KFFM as part of the Metronomics business growth system. Rather than treating cash as a finance problem, they mapped the full flow of value through the business—identifying the key functions that put money in the bank:

- Marketing
- Sales
- Customer Success
- Finance

Each function had clearly defined widgets—leading, non-financial indicators that showed whether the system was healthy long before revenue appeared (or disappeared). Qualified leads. Conversion rates. Onboarding capacity. Days to collect.

The KFFM became more than a diagram. It became the team's shared dashboard.

Every week, the leadership team reviewed the flow together. Red metrics weren't hidden or explained away—they were surfaced early. If customer success started to strain under growth, it showed up immediately. If marketing volume dipped, sales didn't find out three months later—they saw it in real time.

This visibility changed how the team behaved.

Instead of blaming downstream functions, leaders worked together to remove bottlenecks. Instead of chasing lagging revenue numbers, they focused on fixing the widgets that drove cash. And instead of operating in silos, the leadership team began to act like a system.

The impact was profound.

Beanworks grew from roughly **$1 million to $7 million in annual recurring revenue in three years**, while maintaining operational discipline and alignment. That execution confidence—built on a clear cash system—played a critical role in the company's eventual acquisition for **over $100 million**.

Dahl later reflected that the KFFM wasn't just a reporting tool—it was the mechanism that kept the flywheel turning. When the company was acquired and those clear lines of accountability were dismantled, growth slowed almost immediately. The system mattered more than the individuals.

The lesson is simple.

Cash flow isn't something you "watch."
It's something you design.

When leadership teams can see how their actions affect cash—every day, every week—the business becomes proactive instead of reactive. And when the system works without you pushing every lever, you've built something far more valuable than revenue.

You've built freedom.

FREEDOM FACTORS

1. DESIGN YOUR CASH ENGINE

Stop reacting to your bank balance and start mapping how value actually flows through your business. Identify the key functions that create, deliver, and convert value into cash. When you can see the system clearly, you can strengthen it deliberately.

2. TRACK LEADING INDICATORS, NOT JUST REVENUE

Revenue and profit are outcomes. Focus on the non-financial drivers that signal future cash—lead quality, conversion rates, delivery capacity, margin discipline, collection cycles. Use a simple red–amber–green view to spot pressure early and act before cash tightens.

3. MAKE CASH A LEADERSHIP DISCIPLINE

Cash generation is not a finance function. It is a leadership responsibility. Review the system weekly, forecast it quarterly, and treat bottlenecks as shared priorities. Rhythm and accountability turn volatility into predictability—and predictability creates freedom.

CHAPTER 10:
Investing in People Worth Building With

Success in business doesn't come down to strategy or even execution. It comes down to people.

You can have the best plan in the world, but without the right people—people who care, who feel connected, who take ownership—momentum is fragile. Over the years, in my own companies and in working with hundreds of business owners, I've seen a consistent pattern: great businesses are not built by extracting performance from people. They are built by investing in them first.

This chapter is about that investment—why it matters, what it looks like in practice, and how it becomes one of the most powerful drivers of long-term value and freedom.

A Peek Behind the Curtain

One of the privileges of being part of the Small Giants Community is the opportunity to participate in our Passport events, where we go behind the scenes of remarkable businesses. We walk the floors, meet the people behind these successful companies, and experience the "mojo," the business equivalent of charisma that Bo Burlingham described in his book *Small Giants*.

One of my first Passport experiences was a visit to Beryl Health, then owned by Small Giants co-founder Paul Spiegelman. Beryl was a health-care company providing outsourced call center and patient engagement solutions for hospitals. At the time the business was operating out of an old Walmart warehouse that had been converted into a call center. From the outside it wasn't glamorous. But the moment you walked through the doors, you could feel it. That vibe Burlingham describes so well. Mojo. The business equivalent of charisma.

The day we visited, Spiegelman rolled into reception on a Segway to welcome us. It was immediately obvious that something was different at Beryl Health. The receptionist wasn't just a receptionist. She was the director of first impressions. The head of HR, Laura, was the Queen of Fun and Laughter. And HR itself was called the Department of Great People and Fun.

In most organizations, quirky titles or ping-pong tables could be dismissed as gimmicks. But at Beryl they were signals. They told you, instantly, that this was a fun and special place. A place where hierarchy was flattened, where dignity mattered, and where leadership didn't hide behind titles. Spiegelman talks about this in his book *Why is Everyone Smiling?*—the idea that "when management shows its fun side, the whole organization breathes easier." [30] At Beryl, there was a deliberate effort to remove any sense of a "class system."

That philosophy showed up everywhere.

There were themed days—seventies dress-up, pajama days, basketball tournaments. There were comic videos where senior leaders willingly made fools of themselves, being dunked at the annual company party. Not to entertain, but to humanize leadership. To say: *we're in this together.*

Whether you were walking through the door for the first time or applying for a job, you got the message quickly. This is a special place. And people matter here.

What struck me most was how intentional it all was.

Beryl had a culture committee called the **Better Beryl Bureau**. This group completely redesigned the onboarding experience. New employees weren't

---

30   Paul Spiegelman, *Why is Everyone Smiling?: The Secret Behind Passion, Productivity, and Profit* (New York: Brown Books Publishing Group, 2020).

handed a laptop and sent to their desk. They were welcomed—literally. A welcome crew met them at the door on day one.

They ran a **Right Start** program where every new coworker spent time with leaders across the business in their first few weeks. Not just learning *what* Beryl did, but *why* it existed and how their role contributed to that purpose.

Beryl's purpose was simple and powerful: **connecting people to healthcare**.

And people didn't just hear that once during induction. They experienced it. Every system, every ritual, every conversation reinforced how their work mattered.

This reminded me of the NASA janitor story Zach Mercurio often references—the one who says, "I'm helping put a man on the moon." At Beryl, people understood their ladder to the moon. They understood their purpose was connecting people to healthcare.

Spiegelman and his leadership team also created formal mechanisms for listening. There was a **Communications Council**—a small group representing frontline call center employees who met regularly with leadership. These were critical people in the business, and Spiegelman wanted to ensure they had a voice.

Sometimes the feedback was small: water fountains placed directly on the call center floor instead of forcing people to walk to break rooms. Sometimes it was bigger: compensation, workload, wellbeing.

There were committees for wellness, finance, outreach, and life—**Beryl Well**, **Beryl Life**, **Beryl Outreach**, **Beryl Savings**. Not as distractions, but as expressions of a belief: if you invest in people as whole human beings, they show up differently at work.

This is where Spiegelman's *Circle of Growth* comes to life.

The Circle of Growth

Spiegelman didn't set out to build a leadership framework.

In fact, the idea behind what later became known as *The Circle of Growth* emerged not in a strategy session but during a candid conversation on a road trip with his CFO, Pat.

Pat had been skeptical about the level of investment in culture and engagement. From a traditional finance lens, it didn't always add up.

But something shifted after Pat spent time visiting clients and seeing Beryl's people in action.

On that drive, he said to Spiegelman, almost offhandedly, *"I think I get it now."*

What Pat had realized was deceptively simple.

When you genuinely take care of employees—when they feel trusted, valued, and respected—they show up differently. They care more. They stay longer. They go the extra mile for customers. And those customers feel it.

That customer loyalty, in turn, drives stronger financial performance.

And because Beryl was privately owned, those profits could be reinvested back into the people—better tools, better environments, better experiences.

That's when Pat said it out loud.

"It's like a circle."

And it was.

- Employee loyalty fuels customer loyalty
- Customer loyalty fuels profitability
- Profitability funds reinvestment in people
- And the cycle strengthens with every turn

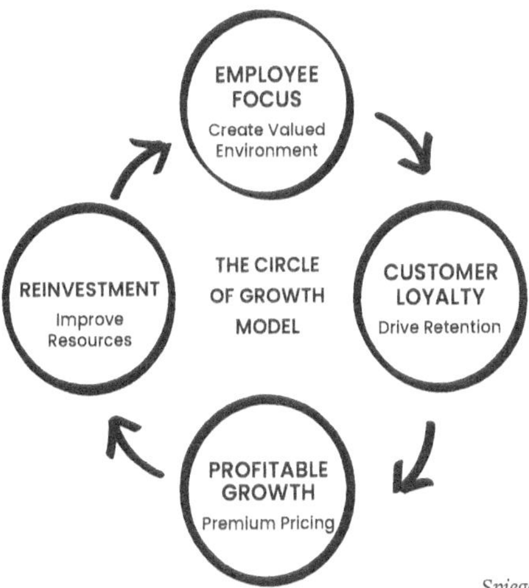

Spiegelman/Beryl Health

What's important here is that none of this was accidental. Spiegelman wasn't being "nice." He was being deliberate. At Beryl, putting people first wasn't framed as a perk or a soft benefit. It was the strategy. It allowed them to charge premium prices in what was otherwise a commodity industry. Clients weren't just buying a service; they were buying consistency, care, and trust—delivered by people who genuinely wanted to be there.

If Culture Isn't Your Default Setting

It's tempting to look at a company like Beryl and think, "That works for Paul. I'm not wired that way."

You may be analytical, operational, focused on numbers and execution rather than energy and engagement. You may not see yourself as a "culture-first" leader.

That's not a problem.
Because culture is not about personality.
It's about alignment.

If values are what you say matter, then culture is how those values are lived. You may have defined your core values and clarified your purpose, but culture is revealed in everyday behavior—how decisions are made, who gets promoted, what gets tolerated, and how conflict is handled. When actions don't match words, people notice. And when they notice that gap, trust and energy begin to erode.

Building culture doesn't require ping-pong tables, free snack bars, or forced fun. Those things are great, but they are not what makes a great culture. Culture is formed and strengthened when you protect standards, address small misalignments early, and reinforce what matters through consistent action. It is built in the quiet moments when people feel cared for and that they matter. Removing the irritations that drain focus, holding firm on values when it's inconvenient, and making decisions that signal, clearly and repeatedly, what this company stands for.

The Squeaky Door

You met Tom Walter from Tasty Catering earlier in the book. When Walter took on the role of chief culture officer, he committed to deepening his understanding of organizational culture and what makes a great culture. Along the way, he got interested in *discretionary thought* and how by removing friction in the work place we can free up discretionary thought.

Walter worked with an industrial psychologist and discovered that the average person has around 60,000 thoughts a day. However, in most workplaces, only a small fraction of those thoughts are directed toward the business. The rest are consumed by noise, interruptions, broken systems, and small frustrations that people learn to endure.

One Saturday morning, Walter was in the office doing one of his regular chores. At Tasty, everyone does something extra. Walter was cleaning the admin and sales area when he found himself wondering about how people experience their workspace. Not in big, obvious ways, but in the small, persistent ones that slowly wear you down.

Earlier that week, during a discussion about friction in the business, someone on the sales team, Jody, had finally said out loud what everyone else had learned to tolerate.

The squeaky door.

Jody's desk was positioned with her back to the entrance of the sales area. Every time someone came in or out, the door swung open and slammed shut. And it squeaked. Loudly.

She told Walter she'd counted it.
One hundred and four times in a single day.

No one had complained before. No maintenance ticket had been raised. It wasn't anyone's formal responsibility to fix it. But that squeaky door, it was constantly distracting Jody. So much so that she counted how often it opened and closed in a day. That door was pulling her attention away from clients, breaking her concentration, and adding a level of irritation that was sapping her discretionary thoughts.

That night, Walter and his brother didn't call a meeting or hand it off to someone else. They fixed the door. They lubricated the hinges, adjusted the closer so it shut quietly, and then went a step further. They reconfigured the space so Jody no longer had her back to the door. Her desk was turned, and a partition with a window was added so she could see movement without being startled by it.

Nothing else changed.
No new targets.
No incentive plan.
No coaching.

The friction was simply removed.

What happened next was unmistakable. Jody's sales didn't improve slowly over time. They jumped. Walter describes it as a sharp, upward angle.

When the door stopped stealing Jody's attention, she got her thinking back and the business benefited.

Protect the Culture You Want

If you say you value respect but allow daily friction or tolerated under-performance to erode focus, your system is sending a conflicting signal. Culture is not the language on the wall. It is the reinforcement of that language through action.

If you think in systems, think of culture as the behavioral output of your values. Your organization constantly transmits signals about what is rewarded, what is ignored, and what is unacceptable. Those signals determine how much ownership people take and how much discretionary effort they invest.

You don't need to become fluffier and more emotional. You need to become more consistent with your values. Culture strengthens when expectations are clear and enforced, when performance issues are addressed early instead of avoided, when dissent is invited rather than punished, and when leadership decisions visibly reflect stated values—even when those decisions are inconvenient or costly.

Many owners who claim they are "not wired for culture" are wired for control. They move fast, solve problems personally, and carry the weight themselves. But culture does not scale through control. It scales through shared values reinforced repeatedly through behavior.

Designing a people-first culture means architecting an environment where your values are lived without your constant intervention. Instead of asking how to motivate people, ask whether your systems reflect what you claim to value. Instead of asking how to make people care more, ask whether someone who shares your values would naturally thrive inside your organization.

Start with the small stuff. Protect your standards. Reinforce what matters consistently.

If you don't design those signals intentionally, misalignment will design them for you.

THE HIDDEN COST OF SETTLING

All the work you do on culture, values, and discretionary effort can be undone if you are not equally intentional about who you bring into the business. You can clarify purpose, reinforce standards, remove friction, and design for dignity, but if you compromise in your hiring, you quietly introduce misalignment. Culture is fragile. One misaligned hire, left unaddressed, can erode months or years of disciplined reinforcement.

When you settle for warm bodies instead of aligned contributors, the cost rarely shows up immediately. It shows up in subtle ways. Your best people begin compensating. Standards soften. Energy shifts from building the future to covering gaps. The very discretionary thinking you worked so hard to unlock begins to disappear. Even talented people, if they are misaligned with your values or the demands of the role, can destabilize a small team.

This is especially true if you are under fifty people. At that size, every hire changes the chemistry of the organization. As Dominic Monkhouse emphasizes, early-stage companies should be aiming for 100 percent A-players, it's not about having a perfect team, but alignment, capability, and accountability.

Hiring must be thoughtful. Onboarding must reinforce expectations clearly. And when you discover a misalignment, you must act quickly. Protecting your culture means protecting your values. If someone doesn't fit even if they might thrive elsewhere, leaving the situation unresolved risks eroding everything you've built.

Making People Matter

Finding the right people is only part of the work. Keeping them engaged requires something deeper than compensation or incentives.

People don't commit to a business because of a mission statement on a wall. They commit when they can see, day after day, how their work contributes to something meaningful, and when they believe they themselves matter within the system.

This is where Mercurio's research becomes so relevant. He makes a deceptively simple point: it's impossible for something to matter to someone who doesn't first believe that they matter. Belonging precedes engagement.

At Beryl, that belief wasn't left to chance. Employees didn't just hear about the purpose of connecting people to healthcare, they experienced it through onboarding, access to leadership, structured listening forums, and decisions that reinforced dignity. The systems told them they mattered.

At Tasty Catering, the same belief showed up in different ways. When employees were invited into conversations about values, and when leadership chose to live those values even when it was inconvenient ownership emerged naturally. Not because it was mandated, and not because it was incentivized, but because it was earned.

When people feel respected, heard, and trusted, they invest more of themselves in the work. They bring attention, care, and judgment to their roles. They protect the customer experience. They raise issues early. They think beyond their job description.

That kind of engagement cannot be extracted. It can only be cultivated.

And over time, it changes the character of the business. Decisions improve. Standards rise. Customers feel the difference. The organization becomes steadier, less dependent on heroic effort, and more supported by shared commitment.

That steadiness has consequences.

It shows up in retention. It shows up in pricing power. It shows up in customer loyalty. And eventually, it shows up in valuation.

That's what keeps great people. Not because they have to stay, but because they want to. And when they stay, build, and care over time, they create something far more important than short-term performance.

They create value.

CASE STUDY: THE RETURN ON INVESTMENT IN PEOPLE

When Spiegelman eventually sold Beryl Health, the outcome might have surprised a lot of people who only understood the business from the outside.

On the surface, Beryl was a healthcare call-center company operating in what most would describe as a commodity market. Plenty of competitors. Similar services. Constant pressure on price. Nothing about it *should* have produced an extraordinary outcome.

And yet, it did.

The business sold for roughly **twenty-two times EBITDA (Earnings Before Interest, Taxes, Depreciation, and Amortization)**, far above what was considered normal in the industry. Not because of clever financial engineering. Not because costs had been slashed at the last minute–in fact Paul had invested heavily in the business prior to the exit, thereby reducing EBITA. But because the business had something buyers struggle to find and rarely trust when they do.

A culture that worked.

Long before the sale, Beryl was already operating differently. Clients were paying **20 to 30 percent more** than competitors—and staying. Profitability was **five to six times higher** than industry norms. Employee turnover hovered around **17 percent** in an industry where **80 percent** churn was common. Client retention sat at around **95 percent**.

Those numbers weren't the result of aggressive sales tactics or short-term optimization. They were the natural outcome of a system that put people first—employees who cared, leaders who listened, and customers who could feel the difference every time they interacted with the business.

Paul often reflects that buyers weren't just acquiring a service. They were acquiring trust. They were acquiring predictability. They were acquiring a business where outcomes didn't depend on heroic leadership or constant oversight, but on people who genuinely wanted to be there and knew why their work mattered.

That's the part many founders, owners and CEOs miss.

Investing in people isn't a feel-good philosophy. It's a value-creation strategy.

It creates businesses that perform better because customers stay. That endure longer because people don't leave. And that are worth more because buyers can see the durability baked into the system.

Because when you get the people part right, everything else doesn't become effortless. But it does become aligned. And alignment, over time, is what turns a good business into a valuable one—and gives the owner the freedom to eventually step away.

FREEDOM FACTORS

1. LIVE YOUR VALUES, DON'T FRAME THEM

Culture is not what you write down, it's what you reinforce. When decisions, promotions, hiring standards, and accountability consistently reflect your stated values, people trust the system. Alignment unlocks energy. Misalignment erodes it.

2. PROTECT THE STANDARD RELENTLESSLY

Small frictions and tolerated misfits quietly drain discretionary effort. Hire carefully. Onboard intentionally. Address misalignment early. Your best people should never have to compensate for weak standards. Culture compounds—in both directions.

3. BUILD DURABILITY THROUGH PEOPLE

When people feel they matter, ownership emerges. When ownership spreads, dependence on you decreases. Over time, that shared commitment creates stability, loyalty, and trust—the kind buyers recognize and pay for. Freedom follows durability.

Part Three: Creating Value

In the first half of this book, we focused on the shift from being at the center of everything to building a high-performing, cohesive leadership team. We exposed the barriers to growth and the importance of alignment.

Now we shift from laying the foundations for growth to increasing business value.

This next section matters whether or not you plan to sell. Building value creates options. It allows you to step back without worrying that everything might unravel. It positions you to respond when an unexpected opportunity appears or when life throws you an unexpected curveball.

In this section, we'll focus on the levers that intentionally increase value: reducing owner dependency, strengthening systems, lowering risk, sharpening differentiation, and building predictable revenue streams. Value does not happen by accident. It is engineered through thoughtful design and consistent discipline.

CHAPTER 11:
Understanding Value Creation

Most business owners believe their company's value is determined primarily by revenue or profit. While these metrics matter, they're only part of the story. I've seen businesses with nearly identical revenues sell for vastly different amounts. The difference isn't the top line. It's how the business is built.

I was one of those owners. When I built my companies, I focused almost exclusively on revenue growth. At the time digitization was exploding across Sub-Saharan Africa. We secured the rights to represent Global 360 (later acquired by OpenText) and expanded rapidly across banking, insurance, logistics, and government. Revenue soared. And the bigger our top line grew, the more successful I believed we were.

Like many entrepreneurs, I saw opportunity everywhere. I spun up new businesses, acquired competitors, launched new products, and expanded internationally. With each move, complexity multiplied, and not just operationally, but structurally. I created an offshore holding company to own our intellectual property and software products. I set up multiple partnerships. I structured intercompany loans. Done properly, this kind of architecture can create efficiency. But mine was a DIY corporate web, designed more for tax optimization than long-term value.

When I finally wanted to step back, the illusion evaporated.

What I had built was worth far less than I expected. Despite impressive numbers, the business was overdependent on me and a couple of key people. Our systems were hardly scalable. And while revenue was climbing, our financial position was precarious at best.

What I had viewed as success was not something attractive to a prospective buyer—at least not the moment they lifted the hood and took a look inside.

This chapter is about understanding why that happens and how to make sure it doesn't happen to you.

THE KEY DRIVERS OF BUSINESS VALUE

In *Built to Sell*, John Warrillow lays out **eight value drivers**[31] that influence what makes a business truly attractive to a buyer and, ultimately, what compels them to pay a premium. Think of these as the core levers you can pull to increase the value of your business, by reducing risk, removing dependence, and demonstrating the businesses growth potential.

1. Growth potential
2. Strength of the management team
3. Financial performance
4. Cash flow
5. Customer satisfaction
6. Unique value proposition
7. Overdependence
8. Recurring revenue

The first four drivers—growth potential, leadership strength, financial performance, and cash flow—form the essential foundations of a strong business. We covered these in the previous section.

BUSINESS VALUE BOOSTERS: THE CORE FOUR

The next four drivers are where value begins to accelerate. These form what I call the Core Four, the levers that most directly increase transferability and reduce risk.

---

31   John Warrillow, *Built To Sell: Creating a Business That Can Thrive Without You* (New York Portfolio, 2012).

1. **Focus on your Core Customer** (**Customer Satisfaction**)

    Designing your business around the needs of your Core Customer increases loyalty, retention, and profitability. It also reduces the risk that comes from chasing the wrong customers.

2. **Build unique differentiators** (**Unique Value Proposition**)

    A clear moat allows you to charge premium prices without racing competitors to the bottom.

3. **Remove dependencies** (**Overdependence**)

    Whether it's reliance on you, key employees, major customers, or critical suppliers, dependencies quietly destroy value. A business that operates without constant heroics is worth more.

4. **Create recurring revenue** (**Recurring Revenue**)

    Stability reduces risk and increases valuation. Predictable revenue also creates freedom: the business stops starting at zero every month.

Together, these four drivers determine whether your business is simply profitable or genuinely transferable.

And this matters even if you never plan to sell.

Building value creates options. It allows you to step back without everything breaking. It strengthens your negotiating position if opportunity knocks. Most importantly, it ensures the business serves your life rather than consuming it.

Value creation is not about planning an exit.
It is about building optionality.

Sell the Future, Not the Past

Before we explore the Core Four value accelerators in depth, one principle must be clear:

Value is created by future potential. Not past performance.

Buyers aren't purchasing what your business did three years ago. They're investing in the cash flow and opportunity it can generate tomorrow.

I once worked with a CEO obsessed with hitting £50 million in revenue. He believed that milestone alone would attract private equity. When I asked what his vision was beyond his £50 million growth goal, what the expansion plan was, what new markets would open, what innovations were in development, he had no answer. The number was the goal.

This reminds me of my own mistake. I was so focused on growing revenue, signing contracts, expanding territories, and adding customers, that I neglected to create a compelling future vision.

Revenue is not a strategy. It's an outcome.

From a buyer's perspective, today's revenue is simply proof of concept. What really matters is a credible vision for future growth.

The company pursuing £50 million had already dominated the European market, but the United States remained largely untapped. Our first move was to research and develop a clear go to market strategy for the U.S.

The new strategy focused on a highly profitable beachhead market with strong pull-through into other tiers. It also centered on building our own brand rather than operating as a white label provider.

The results were so strong that the company has put attracting private equity on the back burner for now.

When the vision for the future shifted from an output to a more strategic growth plan in service of the company's core purpose of "Stopping the World Safely," the value of the business changed. Employees, partners and potential customers were excited by the mission, and that excitement is contagious.

That doesn't mean history is irrelevant. Far from it.

If you're considering a sale in the next twelve to twenty-four months, discipline matters. Clean financials. Clear budgets. Forecasts tracked against results. A pattern of execution. History gives your future credibility.

But history alone doesn't create value. It supports it.

Without a believable future, even strong numbers lose their shine. With a compelling future and a track record of delivery, buyers lean in.

I see this clearly in a client who owns a fast-growing mobile clinic company. What attracts attention isn't just their current performance. It's their vision for the future: making healthcare accessible to underserved communities through a network of mobile healthcare clinics. The numbers matter. But the opportunity for growth, supported by scalable systems, strong leadership, *and* past performance, is what creates buyer confidence.

FREEDOM FACTORS

1. REVENUE IS NOT VALUE

Income can look impressive and still be fragile. Real value is built through structure, leadership, scalability, and independence from the owner. If the business only works because you are at the center, it may generate income but it won't command a premium.

2. BUYERS INVEST IN THE FUTURE

Historical performance builds credibility, but valuation is driven by believable future cash flow. A compelling vision, supported by clean financials and consistent execution, is what turns strong numbers into premium multiples.

3. RISK DETERMINES WORTH

Dependencies on you, on customers, on key employees, and on unstable systems erode value. The more resilient and transferable your business is, the more options and negotiating power you create.

CHAPTER 12:
Customer at the Center

Most business owners are asking the wrong question.

"How do we get more customers?"

It sounds logical. Growth solves everything, right? I used to think that way.

For me, growth was about the next deal. The next contract. The next customer who said yes. Revenue was the scoreboard, and as long as it was moving in the right direction, I assumed we were building something valuable.

What I didn't spend enough time asking was a far more strategic question: *who are we truly built to serve?*

Instead of identifying the type of customer who valued our work most, the ones who appreciated our expertise and were willing to pay for it, we followed opportunity wherever it appeared. If someone needed document storage, we would provide it. If another client wanted imaging software customized for their environment, we would build it. If a new industry showed interest, we would adapt our pitch and go after it.

At the time, I didn't think we were doing anything wrong.

I was relatively inexperienced, and the idea of a Core Customer wasn't something I had fully understood, let alone built strategy around. Growth felt like validation. If someone was willing to pay us, that was enough proof that we were on the right path.

So, we kept saying yes.

What I didn't yet appreciate was the difference between revenue and alignment. We were adding customers, but we weren't asking whether those customers were strengthening the kind of business we wanted to build, or simply consuming time, resources, and energy that could have been invested in the customers who truly valued our products and services.

We were growing, but we weren't growing by design. And over time, that distinction becomes expensive.

You'll probably recognize the pattern by now, the slow drift toward the shiny object, Doom Loop.

Recently, I worked with a 3D printing company serving high-performance industries such as motorsport teams, aerospace engineers, and advanced marine manufacturers. These were demanding customers who value precision, speed, engineering collaboration, and reliability. They are the kind of customers willing to pay a premium for performance because performance truly matters to them.

At the same time, the company was investing in launching an online portal designed to attract smaller, one-off print jobs. The thinking was simple: fill spare capacity, increase machine utilization, generate incremental revenue.

In theory, it made sense. In practice, it introduced complexity.

Marketing now had to attract a completely different type of buyer, one who was more price sensitive, more transactional, and often less familiar with the technical nuances of additive manufacturing. Operations had to manage shorter runs and more variability.

None of this was inherently wrong. But in a small business, resources are finite. Every new initiative competes for attention, energy, and focus. And this one was pulling time and capability away from the company's Core Customer, those high-performance clients who truly valued their expertise and were willing to pay for it.

Contrast that with the hydraulic fluid manufacturer I mentioned in chapter 6. They made the deliberate decision to reduce their bulk, low-margin production and focus on higher-value specialty fluids. Over time, they implemented multiple price increases in a single year and began attracting some of the most respected global brands in their sector, their Core Customers.

That focus on serving a Core Customer didn't expand their market, it narrowed it.

And that narrowing strengthened them.

The idea of focusing on fewer customers feels counterintuitive. When revenue feels uncertain, the instinct is to cast the net wider. Many business owners say yes to almost everything because they're petrified of missing an opportunity.

But that fear often creates the very complexity that weakens the business.

The companies that scale profitably and build enduring value do the opposite. They become crystal clear about one type of customer, the one who values what they do most, pays appropriately for it, and remains loyal because the experience consistently delivers value.

What is a Core Customer?

Just as you must be clear about your purpose and the people you invite onto your team, you must be equally clear about who you are choosing to serve. Because the customer you choose ultimately shapes the business you become.

Without that clarity, different parts of the organization begin pulling in different directions. Sales pursues whatever opportunity appears. Marketing experiments too broadly. Product adapts to fulfill one-off requests. Support reacts to whoever shouts the loudest. Customers are still won, but often through discounting, customization, and effort rather than through clear value alignment.

A Core Customer is the person who **values what you do most** and is **willing to pay a premium** for it.

Having a Core Customer doesn't mean you'll never take work outside that segment. It means you stop *designing your business around everyone.* Your Core Customer becomes the reference point for decisions: strategy, messaging, product development, and the experience you deliver.

Most businesses naturally fall into a bell curve.

In the center are customers who truly fit. They understand your value, require minimal persuasion, and generate strong margins. They tend to stay. They tend to refer.

But here is the critical insight.

In many businesses, the true Core Customers represent a surprisingly small percentage of the total base. Often it is closer to 10 to 20 percent. Yet that small group can account for the majority of revenue and an even greater share of profit.

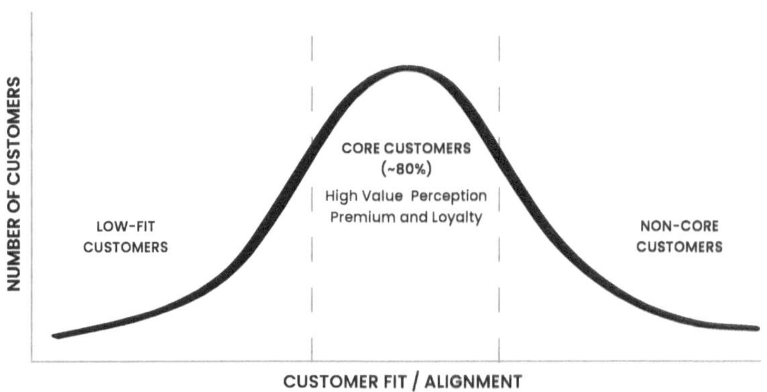

The remaining customers may make up 80 percent of the list, but they do not contribute equally. Many require more hand holding, more discounting, more customization, and more management attention. They generate activity. They generate revenue. But they do not always generate profit and value.

As you move toward the edges, fit decreases. These customers may still buy, but they are often more price-sensitive, more demanding, or require greater adaptation. They generate revenue, but not always value and profitability. If you design your business around them, complexity increases and margins begin to narrow.

The goal is not to eliminate the edges entirely.
The goal is to stop letting them dictate your strategy.

Instead, design for the center. Strengthen your offer around the customers who fit best. Deepen the experience. Refine the messaging. Build systems that serve them exceptionally well.

When you do, something interesting happens. The right customers become easier to attract. The wrong customers become easier to say no to. And the business becomes simpler, more profitable, and more aligned.

The Value of Core Customers

Core Customers don't just produce revenue. They produce predictability. They renew. They expand. They refer. Their behavior stabilizes cash flow and reduces volatility, two things buyers care deeply about. A concentrated base of loyal, well aligned customers increases confidence in future earnings. And confidence drives valuation.

The hydraulic fluids manufacturer I mentioned earlier understood this clearly. They identified the customers who cared most about high-performance specialty fluids, dependable delivery, and product consistency that matched their brand standards. Instead of spreading effort across bulk, lower-margin production, they deliberately narrowed their focus.

They eliminated their bulk fluid line and doubled down on their Core Customer.

Over time, they've attracted some of the most respected global brands in their industry and protected their margins by pushing through several prices increase in a year without those customers leaving.

Revenue did not disappear. Margins expanded. Operational complexity decreased. The business became simpler to run and more attractive to a buyer.

For them, Core Customer clarity was not a marketing exercise. It was a strategic decision about what kind of business they wanted to build and who they wanted to build it for.

Who is *Your* Core Customer?

Robert H. Bloom defines a Core Customer as the *individual* who will buy from your company for *optimal profit*.[32]

The word individual matters in that phrase.

It means identifying the specific person, not just a generic profile, who will ultimately make the decision to purchase from you. This requires specificity. Not "mid-sized manufacturers." Not "enterprise clients."

It requires identifying the individual decision-maker. What are they accountable for? What pressures do they face? What does success look like in their role? Why would choosing you make their job easier, or safer, or more successful?

When leadership teams work through this exercise honestly, they often discover that their best customers share more in common than they realized.

The shift happens when you stop asking, "Who can we sell to?" and start asking, "Who are we built for?"

Defining Your Core Customer

Defining your Core Customer is not just a marketing function. It is a strategic alignment process that should involve your entire leadership team. The process is likely to spark some heated debate, that's a good thing.

---

32   Robert H. Bloom, Dave Conti, *The* Inside Advantage: The Strategy that Unlocks the Hidden Growth in Your Business (New York: McGraw Hill 2007).

What matters is that everyone has the opportunity to contribute and feels comfortable sharing their opinion, and that you walk away aligned.

Again, this isn't a one-and-done process. It may take time, and even some trial and error, before you truly define your core customer. The important part is to do the work and refine your understanding over time.

When I facilitate this exercise with leadership teams, we begin by describing the decision-maker in concrete terms. Not a marketing persona—but a real individual. What is their role? What are they accountable for? What does their week look like? What are their needs?

Then we narrow further. What are the three most important outcomes they need from a partner? Not ten. Not a long list of nice-to-haves. Three benefits that genuinely match their needs.

Finally, we examine our own offering. Which of our capabilities directly serve those priorities? Which features exist because of legacy decisions? Which services were built for customers outside our Core segment?

The exercise often exposes gaps and sharpens our focus on what our Core Customer truly needs from a supplier.

Paradata's "Peter"

When Shannon Byrne Susko led Paradata, she and her team defined their Core Customer with striking simplicity and clarity. They didn't describe a market segment. They described *the* person who valued and was willing to pay for their service.

He was a sales leader in his forties or fifties. Married, with kids. Probably coaching little league on the weekends. Always on his mobile phone. Under constant pressure to hit his numbers. Wishing he could make the same money with less hassle and spend more time with his family (don't we all!).

They named him Peter.

Peter wasn't a marketing persona buried in a slide deck. Susko and her team brought Peter into the room. They created a cardboard cutout of him and gave him a literal seat at the table during planning meetings.

He was not there as theatre or gimmick. He was there as a constant reminder that every decision, every initiative, and every priority had to serve a real person with real pressures and real needs.

If that sounds unusual, consider that Jeff Bezos famously leaves an empty chair in meetings to represent the customer.

Peter sold credit-card merchant accounts, and his needs were simple:

- Making money
- Closing deals quickly
- Avoiding support headaches after the sale

That clarity changed everything.

Instead of adding random features or reacting to competitor noise, Paradata set their sights on building capabilities that made Peter's life easier. Merchant accounts could be set up in under an hour, at a time when the process could take months. The platform was highly reliable. Service was available around the clock. And multiple currencies were supported for customers in other countries.

Their 3HAG, to become the leading North American payment service provider, wasn't a pipedream. It was anchored in serving Peter better than anyone else.

When product debates surfaced, they asked: *Does this help Peter sell more?*
When pricing discussions arose: *Would Peter see the value?*
When hiring: *Will this person strengthen our ability to serve Peter?*

Having that cardboard cutout of Peter at the table was a simple but powerful way to keep the team focused on who their Core Customer was and how their strategy needed to be shaped to serve him well.

Building a Customer-Centric Culture

Over the years, I've noticed something predictable. When leadership teams first commit to narrowing their focus, energy rises. Strategy sharpens. Messaging improves. But then something uncomfortable happens: the customer starts talking back.

And not always kindly.

Most business owners say they want feedback. Far fewer genuinely want to hear it. I've sat in leadership meetings where an employee shares a difficult comment from a customer, only for someone to respond, "They just don't understand what we do." It may feel like a small dismissal in the moment, but the message is clear: we're not *really* interested in customer feedback. Over time, employees stop sharing what they're hearing. They protect themselves instead of protecting the business. And when that happens, a vital feedback loop is lost.

A customer-centric culture doesn't mean you're soft. It means you are willing to sit with discomfort and ask better questions. Where are we creating friction? Where are we missing the mark? Where are we unintentionally making it harder for our Core Customer to win?

Outside of your people, one of the most effective systems for customer feedback is the **Net Promoter Score** (**NPS**), introduced by Frederick Reichheld of Bain & Company33. It's built around one elegantly simple question:

"How likely are you to recommend our product or service to others?"

Customers respond on a scale from 0 to 10. Those who answer 9 or 10 are considered **Promoters**, loyal advocates who actively recommend you. Those who answer 7 or 8 are **Passives**, satisfied but unenthusiastic. And those who answer between 0 and 6 are **Detractors**, customers who are unhappy and may discourage others.

Your score is calculated by subtracting the percentage of Detractors from the percentage of Promoters:

NPS = Percentage Promoters - Percentage Detractors

If 65 percent of your customers are Promoters and 15 percent are Detractors, your NPS is +50.

As a general guide, a score above +50 is considered strong and signals healthy customer loyalty. Scores above +70 are rare and often described as world-class, reflecting a high concentration of customers who don't just buy from you, but actively advocate for you. The higher the score the more valuable your business. And the more likely an acquirer is to pay a premium.

But the number itself is not the point. The point is what the number reveals and what you are willing to do about it. There is little value in running an annual survey and then changing nothing. Tools like NPS need to be woven into the way you operate and used to actively inform your strategy.

---

33   Fredrick Reichheld, "Prescription for Cutting Costs" Bain & Company, Inc (no date provided), http://www.bain.com/Images/BB_Prescription_cutting_costs.pdf, accessed January 20, 2025.

USING FEEDBACK TO DRIVE GROWTH

Regardless of the tool you use—NPS, regular customer interviews, advisory boards, lifecycle surveys, account reviews, or something entirely different—the method matters less than the discipline. What truly matters is that you establish a feedback loop and treat it with seriousness and consistency.

Once feedback is gathered, the real work begins. The next step is to lean in, especially when what you hear feels uncomfortable. That discomfort is often where the insight lives. Ask the follow up questions:

- What made you give us that score?
- What do you value most about working with us?
- Where are we falling short?
- What would meaningfully improve your experience?

In my experience, simply opening that conversation creates enormous goodwill. When a customer senses that you genuinely care, not just about the contract, but about their business and their experience, something shifts. They stop feeling like a transaction and start feeling like a partner.

Listening, however, is only the beginning. The next step is to look for patterns. Individual comments are useful, but patterns reveal structural truth. Friction points need to be surfaced, discussed, and addressed. Decisions must be made about what to fix, what to improve, and what to clarify. Feedback should directly inform your priorities, shaping product development, service standards, communication rhythms, and even hiring decisions that strengthen your core competencies.

When customers see that their input leads to tangible change, even incremental change, trust deepens. And when trust deepens, loyalty strengthens. Over time, that loyalty becomes one of the most durable and valuable assets in your business.

The tool itself is secondary.
The discipline of maintaining the feedback loop is what drives growth.

CASE STUDY: JIBESTREAM—HOW FOCUS FUELED GROWTH

When Chris Wiegand, cofounder of Jibestream, began feeling mounting pressure from his board to deliver stronger results, he knew incremental improvements wouldn't be enough. Revenue was coming in, but performance wasn't where it needed to be. Complexity was slowing them down.

Jibestream specialized in indoor navigation technology—helping people find their way inside complex buildings like hospitals, corporate campuses, airports, and shopping malls. Their client list was impressive. They had worked with organizations ranging from major sports venues to The Pentagon.

But that diversity concealed a structural problem.

Each new client required customization. Different industries had different requirements. The code base had evolved in multiple directions. What was meant to be a scalable SaaS platform had gradually become a professional services business disguised as software.

They weren't building a repeatable engine. They were rebuilding the engine for every customer.

Wiegand and his leadership team made a deliberate decision: reduce complexity at its source. That meant answering a difficult question:

Who are we truly built to serve?

The first step was narrowing the field to three industries where customer needs overlapped: healthcare facilities, corporate campuses, and shopping malls. These organizations shared common characteristics. They already had mobile apps. They needed a mapping engine that could integrate cleanly. They required digitized facility maps and reliable APIs to connect with other systems.

There was commonality—and commonality is what allows software to scale.

From there, the team clarified their Core Customer within those industries: the decision-maker responsible for digital experience and operational efficiency. They committed to becoming exceptional at one thing: putting maps into apps, reliably and repeatedly.

The shift was not painless.

Wiegand had to let go of good customers who didn't fit the new direction. Interesting projects were declined. Short-term revenue was sacrificed in favor of long-term clarity and a shift to Annual Recurring Revenue (ARR). But as resources were redirected toward aligned customers, the business began to change.

Revenue grew by more than **250 percent**.[34] Profitability improved. The product became cleaner. Delivery became repeatable. The company moved from customization-heavy services toward a scalable SaaS model.

Ultimately, Jibestream was acquired by Inpixon—not because it served the widest range of industries, but because it had become focused, scalable, and strategically clear.

They didn't grow by expanding their reach.
They grew by narrowing it.

---

34   PR Newswire, "Unparalleled Growth Trajectory for Jibestream's Indoor Mapping Engine." *PR Newswire*, accessed December 2, 2024.

FREEDOM FACTORS

1. FOCUS CREATES SCALE

When you try to serve everyone, you customize everything. That may grow revenue, but it rarely builds value. Clarity about your Core Customer allows you to standardize, simplify, and scale.

2. REVENUE IS NOT THE SAME AS VALUE

Some customers generate sales. Others generate transferable value. Core Customers stay longer, pay premiums, and allow you to build systems around common needs. That's what buyers trust and what creates freedom for you.

3. COURAGE PRECEDES CLARITY

Narrowing your focus often requires letting go of "good" customers and short-term revenue. That decision can feel risky. But disciplined focus reduces complexity, strengthens margins, and builds a business that grows by design, not by accident.

CHAPTER 13:
Dig a Moat

In the last chapter, we talked about defining your **Core Customer**, the person who values what you do most, is willing to pay a premium, and stays loyal because the experience is genuinely better.

But clarity on *who* you serve is only half the work.

The next question is the one your customer answers every time they renew, reorder, or recommend you:

Why should they choose you... and keep choosing you?

This is where differentiation becomes one of the most powerful drivers of business value. A business that is meaningfully different earns pricing power, attracts loyalty, and becomes harder to replace. And when a company is hard to replace, it becomes far more attractive, whether you're thinking about buyers one day, or simply trying to build a business that doesn't get dragged into constant discounting and churn.

Michael Porter, one of the most influential voices in business strategy, famously said, "Competitive strategy is about being different. It means deliberately choosing a different set of activities to deliver a unique mix of value."[35]

He wasn't suggesting that you avoid challenge. He was pointing to a deeper truth: that valuable businesses don't fight on the same battlefield as everyone else. They compete on different terms; they dig a moat.

---

35   Micheal E. Porter, Jim Collins, and Jerry I. Porras, *HBR's 10 Must Reads on Strategy* (Boston: Harvard Business Review Press, 2011).

The moat is not a single feature or clever slogan. It's the deliberate construction of a small set of meaningful differentiators that, together, make your business hard to copy.

Most business owners, especially in the messy middle of growth, drift into the comparison game. They watch competitors, borrow what appears to be working, and try to be slightly better, faster, or cheaper. The result is predictable: businesses start to look alike, and look-alike businesses compete on price.

A moat is not built through random acts of differentiation. It's built through deliberate strategic choices. You decide what you will be known for, align with your customers' needs, and then building capabilities, systems, and discipline that competitors cannot easily replicate.

That's what this chapter is about.

Why You Need a Moat

At the time of writing this, I'm in Istanbul, once known as Constantinople. When I walk along the Bosphorus, I can still see the remnants of the walls that protected this city for centuries. I've always been fascinated by the way Constantinople was designed to survive.

It wasn't protected by one simple barrier. It had layers.

The famous Theodosian Walls were a massive triple-layered defense system guarding the land approach. The city's strategic peninsula location meant it was protected on multiple sides by sea walls. And across the Golden Horn, there was even a heavy defensive chain, an ingenious obstacle that could stop enemy ships from entering the harbor.

Combined with immense wealth, disciplined armies, and strong naval power, these fortifications made Constantinople close to impregnable in a world of medieval siege warfare.

For centuries, it held.

Until, in 1453, gunpowder and cannons changed the game. The very walls that had protected the city for generations were suddenly vulnerable. Constantinople resisted for 53 days before the walls finally fell on May 29, 1453.

There is a lesson in that story. Do not become overconfident in your differentiation, and do not ignore shifts in your environment.

The strongest businesses are the hardest to besiege. They don't rely on one advantage. They build layers of protection: differentiation, loyalty, systems, and a strategy that competitors can't easily copy. That's what a moat does. It keeps you out of price wars. It protects your margins. It makes you harder to replace.

But unlike Constantinople, your moat cannot remain static. The market changes. Technology evolves. Customer expectations rise. The businesses that win over the long-term don't just build a moat. They continually reinforce and strengthen it.

Of course, your competitors aren't showing up with battering rams and cannons. But the pressure is real. Every industry is crowded, and there will always be someone trying to take your customers by undercutting your price, copying your offer, or shouting louder than you can.

And here's where most business owners go wrong. They respond by playing the comparison game. They obsess over being the best rather than being unique, and almost always that leads to copying a competitor, trying to keep up, or trying to overtake them. Staying aware of your industry is wise. Structuring your strategy around it is exhausting. If you devote too much energy to competitors, you slowly drain your own moat.

There's a different approach. You can replace the comparison game for real strategy.

In a 1996 Harvard Business Review article, Michael Porter describes strategy as being different. He writes, *"It means deliberately choosing a different set of activities to deliver a unique mix of value."*[36]

That word deliberately matters.
Strategy is not reacting. It is choosing.

Building a moat in business means deliberately choosing a set of activities and capabilities that make you genuinely hard to replace. It means aligning those choices with your Core Customer and then reinforcing them consistently. Over time, those reinforcing choices compound. They shape your brand. They influence who you attract. They determine how you price. They simplify decision making.

A Moat is Built with Intention (and Can Crumble)

Let me show you what Porter means in the real world.

For decades, Southwest Airlines was one of the most cited examples of strategic clarity in modern business. Not because it was flashy. Not because it was luxurious. But because the airline made deliberate choices and stuck to them.

At a time when airlines competed on route networks, first-class service, airport lounges, and layered pricing structures, Southwest chose a different game.

Its original Core Customer was what they called the "beleaguered Texas business traveler."[37] These were men flying short-haul routes between Dallas, Houston, and San Antonio. They weren't looking for champagne. They wanted reliability, speed, warmth, and a fair price.

---

36   Michael E. Porter, "What is a Strategy?" *Harvard Business Review* (November,1996) 61-78, https://hbr.org/1996/11/what-is-strategy.

37   Bloom and Conti, *The Inside Advantage*.

Southwest's founders, Rollin King and Herb Kelleher, saw an opening others had ignored.

While Braniff lavished attention on first-class passengers, short-haul business travelers were largely underserved. King sketched the original triangle route on a napkin. Kelleher helped fight the legal battles to make it viable. And together, they built a model around a customer the incumbents had overlooked.

- Point-to-point routes instead of hub-and-spoke.
- Fast turnarounds instead of padded schedules.
- A standardized fleet instead of operational complexity.
- No-frills service that kept costs low, but culture warm.

Even policies that looked quirky were strategic. Open seating sped up boarding. "Bags Fly Free" built trust and simplified pricing. A deeply employee-first philosophy created service that competitors couldn't replicate because it wasn't a script, it was culture.

Their proposition was simple: **"love at low cost."** They wanted to treat the "much abused" business traveler like a human being and at $15 per flight between Dallas and San Antonio.

But differentiation doesn't happen overnight. For decades, Southwest blended cost leadership with focused differentiation. Its structure, culture, operations, and brand all reinforced the same strategic idea. Open seating. No baggage fees. Fast gate turns. A single aircraft type. A playful, human culture. Business schools taught it as a model of strategic alignment—everything fitted together and each differentiator reinforced the other.

That coherence was their moat.
But here is the part that matters for us.
A moat is not permanent.

After forty-eight consecutive years of profitability, Southwest began facing mounting financial pressure. A highly publicized service meltdown in 2022[38] exposed operational vulnerabilities. Activist investors began pushing for structural change. Performance expectations rose. And in 2025 and 2026, Southwest announced what it described as the most ambitious transformation in its history.

The airline began shifting toward more industry standard practices. Assigned seating. Baggage fees. Fare segmentation. Corporate restructuring.

These moves may appear rational. Markets evolve. Pressure mounts. Investors demand returns. But strategically, something subtle happens when you begin copying the industry you once disrupted. You move toward the middle. And the middle is the most dangerous place to compete.

Whether Southwest ultimately regains a renewed form of clarity or successfully evolves its model remains to be seen. But the lesson is timeless.

Your moat is not something you build once and defend forever. It is something you must continually evaluate, reinforce, and, when necessary, redesign.

Pressure will always tempt you toward the middle. Toward what feels safe. Toward what everyone else is doing. But safety in the short term can quietly weaken your strategic position over time.

The businesses that endure are not the ones that never change. They are the ones that evolve deliberately, without surrendering the coherence that made them different in the first place.

Finding Your White Space

Let's return to Paradata for a moment.

In the previous chapter, we met Peter, the reseller who cared about three simple things: making money, closing deals quickly, and never having to

---

38   Kari Tangalakis-Lippert, "Southwest holiday meltdown may be a sign of air travel drama to come," *Los Angeles Times*, January 26, 2023, https://www.latimes.com/business/story/2023-01-26/southwest-holiday-meltdown-may-be-a-sign-of-air-travel-drama-to-come.

deal with support calls after the sale. Peter wasn't a demographic profile. He was a lens. Every strategic decision at Paradata was filtered through him.

But knowing Peter was only the beginning.

The harder question was this: if Peter has options why would he choose Paradata over everyone else?

Shannon Byrne Susko and her team did not start by studying competitors' websites and pricing pages. In fact, I am not even sure competitors had websites or publicly available pricing back then. What they did instead was step back and map the landscape.

Using what they called the Attribution Framework, they identified the key attributes of the market they were operating in. They ranked their own company on a scale of 1 to 5 against each attribute and then repeated the exercise with three or four competitors.

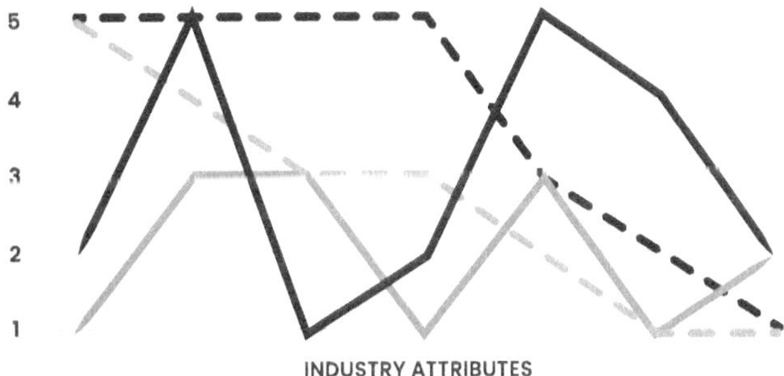

Adapted from 3HAG Way

Along the x-axis the attributes that customers valued: 24/7 Service, Reseller Program, Setup, Multicurrency, Back Office, POS integration, and Merchant accounts. Along the y-axis, a score of 1-5.

When they plotted it out, a pattern emerged.
Most competitors were clustered together.

They were competing on similar dimensions. Similar onboarding timelines. Similar service levels. Similar pricing structures. The map looked crowded.

But there were gaps. There were areas where no one had committed to being decisively better.

That was the white space Susko and her team were after.

For Paradata, the white space wasn't about adding features. It was about eliminating friction for someone like Peter. If Peter's income depended on closing deals quickly, why did merchant setup take weeks? If his reputation depended on reliability, why was support slow or hard to reach?

So, they made a decision. For the next three years, they would build their moat in that white space.

- Answer-the-phone service with real humans, immediately accessible
- A white-label reseller program that gave Peter what he needed
- Merchant setup in less than an hour—at a time when competitors took months
- Multi-currency support, long before it was standard

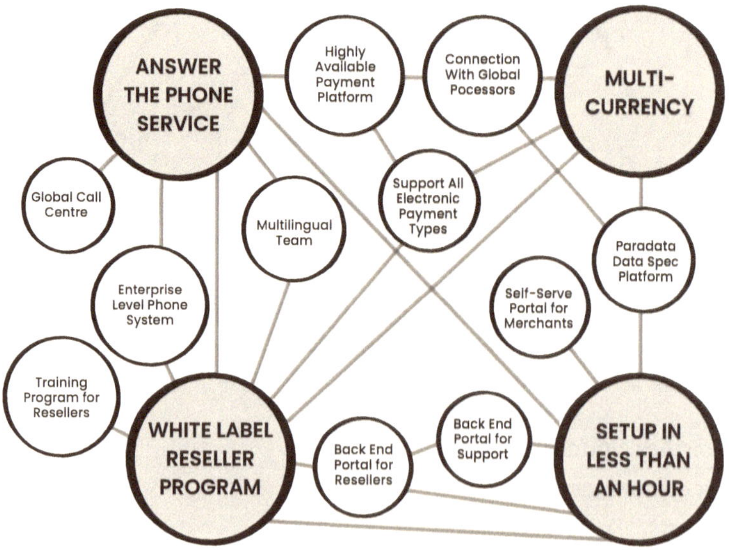

Adapted from Shannon Byrne Susko, Metronomics

None of those capabilities existed off the shelf in 2000. They had to be built. Systems redesigned. Processes simplified. Talent hired. Trade-offs made.

And here's what matters: they didn't try to win everywhere. They didn't attempt to dominate every attribute on the map. They were deliberate, chose their dimension and committed to dominating in those spaces.

Over thirty-six months, quarter by quarter, those choices accumulated. What began as a strategic picture ultimately became operational reality. What began as white space became their moat.

Alignment

This is where everything we've discussed starts to come together.

Earlier in the book, we talked about your long-term direction, your ten-year thinking or BHAG. Then we focused on your three-year picture, the bridge between where you are today and where you want to be. After that, we looked at your Core Customer and what they truly need. Now, we add differentiation.

When these pieces line up, differentiation is no longer something you hope will happen. It becomes something you build on purpose.

Your differentiators define how you will compete and the capabilities you commit to building that make you hard to replace. Your annual and quarterly priorities are the construction plan that turns those commitments into reality.

This is what digging a moat actually looks like. It is not a brainstorm. It is not a rebrand. It is not a marketing refresh. It is a disciplined three-year build schedule.

When Paradata committed to merchant setup in under an hour, that was not just an idea on a slide. It was a clear decision to build a key differentiator that directly served a real customer need. It required developing new technology, hiring skilled software architects and developers, and pushing the limits of what was possible at the time.

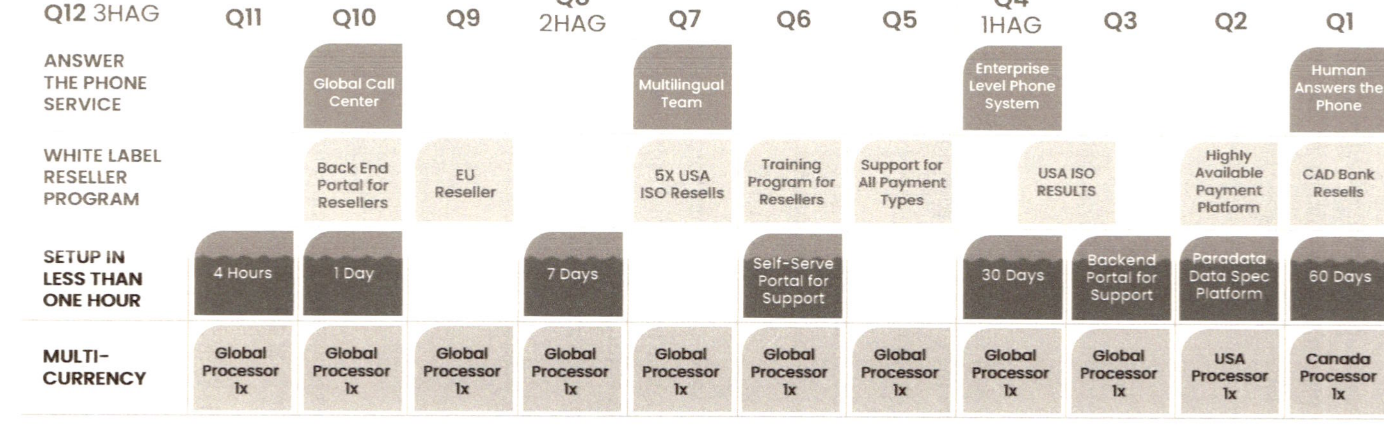

Q12 3HAG	Q11	Q10	Q9	Q8 2HAG	Q7	Q6	Q5	Q4 1HAG	Q3	Q2	Q1
ANSWER THE PHONE SERVICE		Global Call Center			Multilingual Team			Enterprise Level Phone System			Human Answers the Phone
WHITE LABEL RESELLER PROGRAM		Back End Portal for Resellers	EU Reseller		5X USA ISO Resells	Training Program for Resellers	Support for All Payment Types	USA ISO RESULTS		Highly Available Payment Platform	CAD Bank Resells
SETUP IN LESS THAN ONE HOUR	4 Hours	1 Day		7 Days		Self-Serve Portal for Support		30 Days	Backend Portal for Support	Paradata Data Spec Platform	60 Days
MULTI-CURRENCY	Global Processor 1x	Global Processor 1x	Global Processor 1x	Global Processor 1x	Global Processor 1x	Global Processor 1x	Global Processor 1x	Global Processor 1x	Global Processor 1x	USA Processor 1x	Canada Processor 1x

Adapted from Shannon Byrne Susko, Metronomics

When they committed to answering the phone with a live human being, it required investing in an enterprise phone system, a knowledge base, and recruiting multilingual team members who could support customers around the clock.

One quarter might focus on building a self-serve portal for merchants. Another on integrating currency capabilities. Another on recruiting a multi-lingual team.

Each quarter built on the one before it, steadily strengthening their core differentiation and deepening their moat. Over thirty-six months, those focused priorities accumulated into real structural advantage.

This is where many leadership teams begin to drift. They set a bold, long-term ambition. They define a clear three-year goal. They even identify meaningful differentiators. But then quarterly execution fills up with reactive work. Operational noise. Short term pressures. Incremental improvements that do not reinforce the moat.

If your quarterly priorities are not strengthening your differentiators, you are not digging your moat. You are simply staying busy.

True alignment means that every quarter you can point to tangible progress that makes you more distinct, more valuable to your Core Customer, and harder to copy. That is when strategy stops being a document and starts becoming architecture.

And when that architecture compounds over time, value compounds with it.

A Closing Thought

When your Core Customer is clear, you stop chasing everyone. When your white space is defined, you stop copying competitors. And when your differentiators are embedded in your three-year plan, you stop reacting to the market and start shaping your position within it.

This is how businesses move from being busy to being easier and more valuable.

A strong moat protects you from price wars. It gives you margin. It stabilizes loyalty. It reduces volatility. And over time, it makes your future revenue more predictable—which is exactly what buyers, investors, and even lenders are quietly assessing.

But a moat is never finished.

Constantinople held for centuries because its defenses evolved, until they didn't. Markets shift. Technology accelerates. Customer expectations change. A differentiator that once set you apart can become industry standard faster than you expect.

The discipline, then, is not simply to build a moat, but to keep reinforcing it.

And there's an important nuance here.

Even the strongest moat cannot compensate for structural fragility. If your business depends heavily on one person, one customer, one supplier, or one key employee, differentiation alone will not protect you. You may be unique, but you are not resilient.

That's where we go next.

FREEDOM FACTORS

1. DIFFERENTIATION IS BUILT, NOT DECLARED

A moat forms when your long-term ambition, three-year goals, and quarterly priorities consistently reinforce a small set of capabilities that competitors struggle to copy.

2. WHITE SPACE REQUIRES COMMITMENT

Finding a gap in the market is not enough. Value compounds when you commit to building into that space for years, even when short-term opportunities tempt you elsewhere.

3. A MOAT MUST BE REINFORCED

Customer expectations shift. If you are not deliberately strengthening what makes you distinct, your differentiation will erode—and so will your value.

CHAPTER 14:
Be Switzerland

At the time of writing, I'm living in Switzerland.

It's a country that has mastered something most business owners struggle with: independence.

Switzerland didn't join either World War. It waited until 2002 to join the United Nations, and only after a national referendum. It trades globally, yet avoids being pulled too deeply into any single alliance, ideology, or power bloc. That posture has not made it weak. It has made it stable, prosperous, and difficult to destabilize.

Switzerland's strength doesn't come from isolation. It comes from balance. Strong relationships combined with clear boundaries. Global engagement without overdependence.

That's exactly what you want for your business

In fact, John Warrillow calls it "The Switzerland Structure."[39] A company becomes more valuable when it isn't overly dependent on any single constituency, whether that's you as the owner, a key employee, one major customer, or a critical supplier.

Because every dependency is risk, and risk reduces value.

When buyers evaluate your business, they're scanning for those risks.

- Can it run without you?

- Would it wobble if one customer left?

---

39   John Warrillow, "A Lesson From the World's Richest People", *Inc Magazine* (7 July 2011), https://www.inc.com/articles/201107/a-lesson-from-the-worlds-richest-people-switzerland.html, accessed November 15, 2024.

- Does key knowledge live in one person's head?
- Is the business model exposed to one supplier?

In this chapter, we'll look at four common dependency traps that quietly erode value, and more importantly, how to dismantle them. Because independence isn't just about valuation.

It's about freedom.

Owner Overdependence

I never got the dreaded vacation call.

You know the one. You're finally away. The sun is warm. Your shoulders have just begun to drop. For a few hours, you almost remember who you were before payroll and strategy and performance reviews filled your head.

And then the phone rings.

Something's wrong. A deal is wobbling. A client is upset. A decision can't be made without you.

I never got that call because I never took the vacation.

For years, I told myself I was simply being responsible. I cared deeply about our customers. I enjoyed being in the room for important conversations. I believed the business needed my judgment to navigate complexity. And to be fair, in the early years, it probably did.

But what starts as necessary involvement becomes insidious dependence.

By the time I began talking to buyers for my information management business, I had built something successful, but deeply reliant to me. I was central to key account relationships. I was involved in pricing and contract negotiations. Clients typically wanted to see me in the room, because I made the decisions.

When buyers looked at the business, they saw potential. But they also saw risk, so they wanted me committed for five years.

Five years! I wanted out.

My plan had been to sell, transition for twelve months, and move into the next chapter of life. Instead, I was looking at a future where I became an employee because I had built a company that couldn't operate without me.

This is one of the most common value killers. The owner becomes the business. And the more indispensable you are, the more fragile the company becomes, and the harder it is to sell or step away from.

It also shapes deal structures in ways many founders don't anticipate.

A buyer may agree on a headline valuation. But once they detect owner dependence, the deal changes. More earn-out. More seller notes. Longer transition periods. They aren't being difficult. They're protecting themselves from the risk that when you step back, performance steps down.

So, instead of paying you upfront based on projected performance, they tie a larger portion of the purchase price to future results. If revenue dips after you sell, you absorb part of the downside. If key customers walk, if the team stumbles, if execution slows, your payout shrinks. Seller notes (or seller financing) can extend that exposure even further, keeping your capital tied to the health of a business you no longer control.

The value of a deal can also decline during due diligence, as the buyer begins to uncover gaps or weaknesses in the business.

Paul Spiegelman experienced this firsthand when he was negotiating the sale of Beryl Health to a private equity firm.[40] The initial valuation and deal terms shifted as the firm uncovered areas that made them uneasy. One of the issues identified during diligence was an overreliance on Spiegelman in sales and marketing. From the buyer's perspective, too much of the company's growth engine rested with Spiegelman and one long-term salesperson.

---

40   Jean Moncrieff, "Episode 27: Culture as Strategy: How Purpose and Values Drove a 22X Valuation with Paul Spiegelman," *The Freedom Experience with Jean Moncrieff* (2024), https://www.jeanmoncrieff.com/podcasts/the-freedom-experience-with-jean-moncrieff/episodes/2148894952 accessed November 15, 2024.

That concentration did not diminish the overall strength of the business. But it did introduce vulnerability. And vulnerability, in the eyes of a buyer, translates directly into risk.

Even if you never plan to sell, owner dependence traps you.

You can't take a real holiday. You hesitate to empower your team fully because you're worried they'll make the wrong call. Clients default to you, which feels flattering at first and exhausting later. Decision-making funnels upward and over time, your team's confidence erodes because you've trained them to wait.

This dependence creates what's commonly referred to as golden handcuffs. You build a successful business, but you're so essential to its operation that you can't step away. You become the linchpin, and removing the linchpin feels dangerous.

Owner Dependence

Reducing owner dependence starts with a shift in mindset. You must move from being the center of everything to building something that doesn't require you to be. That means letting go of the belief that you're the only one who can close the deal, solve the problem, or make the final call. If you cling to that identity, no structure will save you.

If you want freedom, you need to build a strong (A-player) leadership team. That starts by shaping the business not around who you are today, but around what your business looks like in the future. Look ahead two years and ask: what does this company require to get there and where am I the weakest link right now?

Most owners wear too many hats. To increase the value of your business, you have to start handing those hats to A-players or Super Whos who can own them fully.

In my case, that means sales and finance. I am not wired for either. So those are the first roles I prioritize when building a business. I look for people who are exceptional in those functions and who understand the path we need to follow to scale and reach our three-year goal quickly.

That shift alone reduces dependency and increases value.

Customer Dependence

In the early days, my business had a healthy mix of clients. Twelve to fifteen key customers and a bunch of smaller ones. None contributing more than ten percent of revenue. It felt balanced, stable, and healthy.

That's the golden rule of customer concentration: **never let one customer account for more than 10 percent of your revenue.**

There's a reason seasoned entrepreneurs talk about the "ten percent rule." When no single customer represents more than ten percent of your revenue, you can lose one and survive. You might feel it, but you won't collapse.

Then we broke that rule.

Our imaging and document storage business landed what seemed like a dream account. It accelerated our path toward $20 million in revenue. I remember the excitement. The validation. The sense that we had harpooned a whale.

But big accounts require resources and can add complexity.

To deliver for this financial services client, we had to triple the size of our team. We had to invest in new equipment and infrastructure. And we had to setup shop in a new city. Essentially, the business moved into orbit around the needs of a single customer.

Within a short period, the client represented more than 30 percent of our total revenue.

And then they hit cash flow trouble.

Suddenly, our whale of a client became a giant anchor dragging us underwater. Every month turned into a scramble. We'd chase clients to make payroll, stretch supplier payments a far out as we could, and sell like lunatics in between to bring in cash to cover costs.

Strategy disappeared. Survival took over.

Ryan Tansom describes a similar experience in his family's copier business.[41] They had $240,000 in payroll every two weeks. As he put it, "The game was to never miss that." When one or two customers carry too much weight, meeting payroll becomes the overriding strategy. Nothing else matters.

That is the real danger of customer concentration. When one client becomes too large, they gain leverage. Your negotiating power weakens. Your hiring decisions begin to revolve around their needs. Your investment priorities shift in their direction. Whether intentionally or not, they start shaping the future of your business.

When a client approaches 15 percent of revenue, it deserves attention. When they move beyond 20 percent, it demands action.

Reducing customer dependence is not about turning away large clients. It is about being disciplined in how you grow. That may mean setting limits on account size, ensuring no single industry dominates your revenue mix, or refusing to make major infrastructure investments unless they serve multiple customers. Defining your Core Customer and narrowing your niche are powerful ways to avoid drifting into overreliance.

It also requires resisting the emotional pull of the whale. Big accounts feel exciting. They create momentum and validation. But a diversified customer base creates resilience. It strengthens your negotiating position. It gives you breathing room. It lets you sleep at night.

---

41   Jean Moncrieff, "Episode 25: Understanding the Game of Ownership with Ryan Tansom," *The Freedom Experience with Jean Moncrieff* (2024), https://www. jeanmoncrieff.com/podcasts/the-freedom-experience-with-jean-moncrieff/ episodes/21488872.

A concentrated customer base may accelerate revenue.

A diversified customer base builds value.

And over the long run, value wins.

Employee Dependence

Overdependence on key employees is another value killer.

Sometimes it's a top-performing salesperson who "owns" the biggest accounts. Other times it's a technical expert who built the core system and knows it better than anyone else. In the early days, these people feel indispensable because, frankly, they were.

In the nineties, when we were building our web content management business, we had a developer who held us over a barrel. He was brilliant. He also knew it. Over time, the requests escalated—more money, a high-performance car, more equity, a seat at the table. That might have all been fine, but he didn't play well with others. He created tension inside the team. But we tolerated it because we believed we couldn't pull it off without him.

That belief gave him power.

I've seen the same pattern play out many times since. Recently, I worked with a company that had to rewrite its entire software platform because one developer had become the sole keeper of critical knowledge. When he left, the business was exposed. No matter how talented someone is, no business should be held hostage by one employee.

You can usually spot the warning signs. Critical knowledge sits with one person. Key conversations can't be had without that individual present. Knowledge isn't documented. There's no person as a backup when they're away. And occasionally, someone begins negotiating from a place of "you can't afford to lose me."

The emotional complexity is what makes this hard.

Often, the person you're dependent on stood with you in the early days. They helped build the company. They sacrificed. They believed when others didn't. Letting go, or even redefining their role, can feel like betrayal.

But businesses evolve.

The people who got you here may not be the people who can take you forward. If someone is no longer an A-player (remember, consistently living core values always matters more than simply exceeding performance expectations) in the current version of your business, they can negatively impact your culture and become a risk. Not because they're bad. Because the demands of the next chapter are different.

Reducing employee dependence means reducing reliance on any single person.

That starts with defining the roles your business needs over the next two or three years to move you toward your goal. It's not about fitting a role to accommodate your existing employees. When a role is clearly defined—mission, accountability, outcomes, values—you can look for the right person to fit that role.

Removing dependence at employee level also means building internal capacity. People and leadership development aren't "nice to haves." It's insurance. If there's no one ready to step up when someone leaves, you don't have depth, you have exposure.

The strongest companies I know are always recruiting values-aligned talent. Not urgently. Not reactively. Continuously. They are building capability ahead of need.

Employee dependence breaks when you stop organizing the business around people and start organizing it around roles, standards, and values.

That shift doesn't just increase value.
It gives you room to lead without fear.

Supplier Dependence

Perhaps the most painful lesson I learned about overdependence came from our software business.

At the time, we were the reseller of a business process management platform across Sub-Saharan Africa. We had built strong relationships with banks, insurers, and government agencies. Revenue was growing. The future looked good.

Then our primary supplier was acquired.

The new owners reviewed their global partnerships and, without as much as a meeting, canceled our contract. They already had an existing partner in our region. We were no longer required, and I received a letter stating that going forward all sales and renewals would go through another company.

Just like that, a significant portion of our business evaporated.

It didn't matter how well we had served customers. It didn't matter how strong our local brand was. We had built our model around one supplier, and they held all the power.

Supplier dependence often hides behind something positive: loyalty.

In the Small Giants Community, one of the defining characteristics of great companies is their **deep, meaningful relationships with suppliers**. These relationships create trust, consistency, and shared growth. You *want* that intimacy. It's part of what makes values-based businesses so strong.

But intimacy and loyalty shouldn't mean vulnerability.

The moment your business relies on one supplier for a mission-critical input—technology, raw materials, logistics, key components—you have handed them leverage over your future. If they change pricing, get acquired, hit capacity limits, alter strategy, or decide to serve your competitors directly, you are exposed.

The goal is not to treat suppliers as interchangeable commodities. The goal is to combine strong relationships with structural resilience.

That begins by identifying your single points of failure. What contracts, platforms, or materials would cause serious damage if they disappeared tomorrow? Technology vendors are a common blind spot. So are exclusive distribution agreements and specialized manufacturing inputs.

Once you see the risk, the work becomes practical.

For anything mission-critical, you need alternatives. Not dozens. Two or three viable options. You don't need to split your volume evenly, but you do need optionality. You want the ability to shift without panic.

The hydraulic fluids manufacturer I worked with did this well. They built deep, long-term supplier relationships—true partnerships—but they also ensured that for any critical raw material or service, alternatives existed. If one supplier faltered, they could pivot without compromising quality or delivery. Their customers never felt the disruption.

They were loyal. But they were not exposed.

The other discipline is architectural. Avoid building your entire infrastructure around one supplier's ecosystem if you can help it. Long-term contracts, internal capability, diversified sourcing, these aren't defensive moves. They are strategic ones.

Breaking the Chains of Dependency

Think about why you started your business in the first place.

For most entrepreneurs, it wasn't purely financial. Yes, money matters. But beneath that was something deeper: the desire for autonomy. The ability to choose your direction. To build something meaningful. To shape your life.

And yet, over time, many of us build businesses that quietly remove that freedom.

I certainly did.

From the outside, our companies looked strong. Revenue was growing. We were expanding. But underneath, the structure was fragile. I was central to key relationships. A few customers carried too much weight. Critical knowledge sat with specific employees. Our model relied heavily on one supplier. Each of those dependencies made the business more exposed than it appeared.

You don't always feel that exposure day to day, but you feel it when something shifts. Your most important customer runs into trouble or finds another supplier. A key person on your team suddenly leaves. A supplier changes the game. Or a potential buyer starts asking hard questions.

That's when you realize the how overdependence can cripple your business.

This isn't only about selling. It's about having options.

A business that can operate without constant intervention gives you the ability to step back, take a real holiday, or explore what comes next, without everything wobbling in your absence.

FREEDOM FACTORS

1. EVERY DEPENDENCY REDUCES VALUE

Whether it's you, a major customer, a key employee, or a single supplier, concentration creates risk. Buyers discount it. Stress increases because of it. And your freedom shrinks in proportion to it.

2. INDEPENDENCE IS BUILT INTENTIONALLY

Reducing dependency doesn't happen by accident. It requires building an A-player leadership team, diversifying revenue, spreading critical knowledge, and creating supplier resilience.

3. RESILIENCE CREATES REAL FREEDOM

A business that can run without constant intervention gives you options. You can step away for a holiday, navigate a downturn, or sell on your terms. Value and freedom rise together when the business no longer hinges on any single point of failure.

CHAPTER 15:
Create Recurring Revenue Streams

Along with reducing dependencies, one of the best ways to increase the value of your business is to make your revenue more predictable.

Predictability reduces risk. And risk is what buyers discount.

When someone looks at your company—whether it's a potential acquirer, an investor, or even a bank—they are trying to answer one question: *how certain is the future cash flow?* The more certain it feels, the more valuable the business becomes. The less certain it feels, the more they protect themselves.

I came to understand this when I acquired my largest competitor, Integrear Systemflo. The CEO, Thomas Hill, was preparing for his next venture and selling off the subsidiaries of a publicly listed group. One of those subsidiaries was a direct competitor of ours.

Hill had built a solid client base over the years. But what struck me most was not just the size of the accounts. It was the strength of the recurring revenue. Every month, a steady stream of income flowed into the business, supported by a small team of just three people.

He approached me about selling almost a year before the deal finally happened. At the time, I simply didn't have the capital to buy him out, so nothing progressed.

Instead, we met for breakfast every now and then. We'd talk about our businesses, compare notes on the market, and inevitably the subject of the acquisition would resurface. Each time, I had to say the same thing: I didn't have a couple of million sitting around to invest in another company. The interest was there. The timing wasn't.

Over those months, I sensed a change in him. His desire to sell the business was becoming more urgent. His attention had shifted. He was already thinking about his next venture in agriculture, and the technology business felt like something he had emotionally left behind.

Then one morning an email landed in my inbox. Hill had outlined a structure that made the deal workable. He would retain the accounts receivable for twelve months if I assumed the accounts payable to our common software vendor.

Those breakfasts mattered more than I realized at the time. They built trust between us. And we also had a strong relationship with the supplier. They understood the quality of Hill's recurring revenue and the stability of the contracts behind it. When I asked for extended credit terms to make the deal possible, they were supportive.

The acquisition added nearly 10 million in recurring revenue to the business and, once we had worked through the accounts payable, it gave us the cash flow we needed to expand into document storage and begin developing our own software products.

But the real value wasn't just in the additional revenue. It was in what I learned by looking closely at how Hill had built his company.

When we opened the books, I realized I had been kidding myself. I thought I understood recurring revenue.

In reality, most of my contracts were still transactional. We had strong relationships and worked with the same clients year after year, but the work itself was project-based. We would win an engagement, deliver it well, invoice, and then begin the cycle again. It was the same client base, but every piece of revenue still had to be re-won. It was steady only because we worked relentlessly to keep it steady.

Hill had built something different. His income did not depend on restarting the sales process every time. It arrived month after month with far less friction. That predictability changed the entire feel of the business. There was less scrambling, fewer last-minute pushes, and greater confidence in the numbers. You could plan. You could invest. You could think beyond the next invoice.

And on top of that stable recurring base, there was additional project revenue layered in, creating upside without constant pressure.

The deal also taught me something about acquisitions. I had always assumed transactions were primarily about valuation models and clever structures. They matter, of course. But this one only worked because I had taken the time to understand what Hill really wanted.

It was not really about the money. His focus had shifted, and all he wanted was to begin his next chapter. Had I understood that sooner, the deal might have moved more quickly. In the end, we structured an agreement that aligned with his priorities while protecting mine.

Ironically, within five years, I found myself in a similar position to Hill. I was ready for my own next chapter, with one foot already out the door.

If you ever find yourself buying a business, remember this: you are not negotiating with a spreadsheet. You are sitting across from a human being with fears, ambitions, and a future in mind. The better you understand that future, the more likely you are to craft a deal that works.

And that brings us back to recurring revenue. Predictable income does more than smooth cash flow. It changes how your business is perceived and gives you real options.

I never asked him directly, but I suspect Hill wanted to sell to me. He cared deeply about his people and his clients, and he knew that I would too. Because of the stability created by that recurring revenue, he was not under pressure. He could afford to wait until we structured a deal that worked for both of us.

Stepping Off the Sales Treadmill

The real power of recurring revenue isn't just found in a higher multiple at exit. It's found in the way the business feels to run.

Without it, many owners live month to month. The calendar turns and the revenue counter resets. You start again, chasing the next deal to cover payroll, overhead, and growth. Even in a healthy business, there's a hum of pressure underneath it all. Sell. Close. Deliver. Repeat.

Carl Saunders described this as living on "diving catches"—those last-minute deals that bring cash in the door and where the team barely knows what's been promised or how it will be delivered. The contract lands, everyone scrambles, the work somehow gets done, and the team celebrates.

Then it starts all over again.

There's energy in that kind of business. It can even be fun for a while. But it doesn't scale well. It doesn't transfer well. And ultimately, it becomes exhausting for the people involved.

Recurring revenue changes the rhythm. When a meaningful portion of your revenue is already committed before the month begins, the tone shifts. Decisions become less reactive. Planning becomes more deliberate. You're not selling from anxiety; you're building from stability.

Instead of living on adrenaline, you create space—space to improve systems, develop leaders, deepen customer relationships, and make thoughtful investments. The business stops feeling like a treadmill and starts feeling like an asset.

Why Recurring Revenue Matters

Recurring revenue transforms your business in three powerful ways:

1. **It reduces risk**

   When a meaningful portion of next month's revenue is already committed, uncertainty drops. Buyers see that immediately.

Stable revenue is easier to underwrite than hope. And when risk drops, so does the discount a buyer applies to your valuation.

2. **It increases trust in the future**

    John Warrillow writes in *The Automatic Customer* that subscription businesses often command higher multiples because buyers are purchasing future cash flow, not just a history of sales.[42] Recurring revenue makes that future visible. It shows patterns, behavior, loyalty. It tells a story about what is likely to happen next. Recurring revenue makes that future easier to trust.

3. **It makes growth easier to fund and manage**

    When you're not chasing new deals from quarter to quarter, you can invest more confidently. You hire with those A-players, invest in your systems, and deepen customer experience. You move from survival mode to growth mode.

Recurring Revenue Isn't Just for Tech Companies

Many business owners assume recurring revenue belongs to technology companies. It doesn't.

Almost every business has recurring revenue hiding inside it. You just need to uncover it. Start by asking:

- What do customers buy repeatedly?

- What do they need regularly?

- What do they outsource because they don't want the hassle?

- Where do they want convenience, consistency, or peace of mind?

- What part of what you do could become an "always-on" service instead of a one-off project?

---

42   John Warrillow, *The Automatic Customer: Creating a Subscription Business in Any Industry* (London: Penguin Random House UK, 2015).

Recurring revenue can show up as:

- subscriptions
- retainers
- service agreements
- maintenance plans
- licensing
- memberships
- ongoing advisory
- bundled packages delivered monthly or quarterly

I'm seeing veterinarians who offer wellness plans for pets. Roofing companies that sell preventative maintenance packages for a recurring monthly fee. Even dentists are in on the game. They all recognize the opportunity to a reliable flow of income.

The Psychological Shift

Moving to recurring revenue isn't just a billing model decision. It's a mindset shift. You must come to terms with the idea that focus is more powerful than a widely cast net. When you do that, you can become more surgical about the products and services you create for your niche.

In earlier chapters, we spoke about your Core Customer and your Key Function Flow Map. This is where those ideas become more practical. Recurring revenue only works if your entire business can deliver consistently.

The KFFM supports a recurring revenue model because it gives you the full picture—from lead generation to onboarding, from delivery to renewal. It exposes weak handoffs. It highlights where work gets stuck. It shows you whether you're building a smooth operation or if there are bottlenecks your team needs to address.

Recurring revenue is not created by clever selling. It's earned through reliable delivery and a great customer experience.

If you're a roofing company offering a preventative maintenance contract and selling peace of mind, you'd better have the systems to back it up. That means someone shows up (KFFM: number of on-schedule checkups) a couple of times a year to clear the gutters, inspect the flashing, and check the integrity of the roof.

And when you combine that with a disciplined feedback loop (KFFM: NPS score), whether that's NPS or another structured feedback approach, you stop guessing about customer satisfaction. You see patterns. You remove friction. You create strong, sticky relationships and customer evangelists.

And so, the question shifts from, "How do we close the next deal?" to "How do we create ongoing value that keeps customers coming back?"

That is the real psychological shift. Recurring revenue is not a billing structure. It is a relationship structure.

Building Value Through Customer Relationships

In a transactional business, every sale feels like a fresh audition. You win the deal, deliver the work, send the invoice, and return to the top of the funnel.

It can be exhausting.

In a recurring model, the sale is the beginning of a longer story. The focus moves from acquisition to retention. You begin to measure churn. You study customer lifetime value. You pay attention to onboarding and service quality in a way you never did before.

And something subtle happens. The business improves.

Because when customers stay longer, you understand them better. You serve them more efficiently. They trust you. They refer you. The relationship deepens, and profitability often improves without dramatic increases in effort.

Recurring revenue doesn't just stabilize cash flow.
It encourages you to build a better company.

CASE STUDY: THE SYSTEM BEHIND SCALE

You'll remember Catherine Dahl from earlier in the book. When she took over as CEO of Beanworks, the company had early traction—but growth was still dependent on hustle. Deals were being won in the classic startup way: through founder energy, urgency, and sheer determination.

Dahl recognized that the business needed flow. Not just sales, but a connected system linking marketing, onboarding, product, and customer success. She introduced a disciplined operating rhythm and began tracking leading indicators daily. Not to control people, but to reduce surprises.

The goal was simple: make growth repeatable.

Over time, the culture shifted. Instead of relying on individual brilliance, the company relied on clarity and accountability. Recurring revenue began to behave predictably because the underlying system was sound.

In three years, Beanworks grew from under $1 million in annual recurring revenue (ARR) to roughly $7 million ARR and ultimately sold for over $100 million.

The exit wasn't just the result of growth. It was the result of *transferability*. Dahl didn't build a business that needed her to survive, she built a high-performing business with growing recuring income. Buyers saw a system that could continue without Dahl at the center. They saw retention. They saw predictability. They saw opportunity.

FINDING HIDDEN OPPORTUNITIES

Recurring revenue often lives inside your existing offer.

A commercial printer can manage branded materials monthly rather than printing on request. A service provider can shift from reactive "break-fix" work to proactive managed services. A consultant can turn one-off workshops into ongoing advisory relationships.

Look at businesses outside your industry for inspiration. Mechanics offer maintenance plans. Roofers sell annual inspections. Pool companies prefer monthly cleaning contracts to emergency rescues.

In each case, the customer isn't buying a transaction. They're buying continuity and peace of mind.

The opportunity isn't to invent something artificial. It's to ask: where does my Core Customer value ongoing support more than occasional intervention?

THE TRANSITION PROCESS

Shifting to recurring revenue doesn't require tearing your business apart.

Start with your best customers. The ones who already trust you. Have honest conversations about what frustrates them. What risks keep them awake? What tasks feel repetitive or distracting?

Design a recurring offer that solves a recurring problem.

Make the value obvious. Be clear about what they receive each month and why it matters. Show how it saves time, reduces risk, or simplifies life.

Then build the supporting systems. Billing. Onboarding. Service processes. Visibility into performance. Use your KFFM to ensure sales, delivery, and service are aligned.

Test with a small group. Gather feedback. Refine before you scale.

MEASURING SUCCESS

To build a recurring revenue engine, you need to track different signals than traditional sales.

Here are the key indicators:

- **MRR (Monthly Recurring Revenue):** predictable monthly revenue

- **ARR (Annual Recurring Revenue):** your annual run rate
- **Churn:** how many customers leave
- **Customer Lifetime Value:** what a customer is worth over time
- **Net Revenue Retention:** how much your existing revenue base grows

If this feels like a lot, start with three: MRR, churn, and NRR. Those three will tell you whether customers are staying, leaving, or deepening their relationship with you.

CREATING STICKY RELATIONSHIPS

The most successful subscription businesses don't just sell products or services—they create ecosystems that become integral to their customers' operations.

Consider how HubSpot evolved from a simple marketing tool into the operating backbone of thousands of companies.

In our case, almost everything runs through it. Our website, sales pipeline, marketing automation, invoicing, customer communication, even elements of support—all connected in one system. And it costs us only a few thousand dollars a month.

Leaving wouldn't just mean switching software. It would mean unwinding the way the business functions. That's what sticky recurring revenue really looks like.

Think about what truly makes customers stay: it's rarely the contract. It's that leaving would mean giving up something valuable.

GETTING STARTED

Look for one opportunity.

One product customers buy regularly. One service they need consistently. One area of expertise you could package. One ongoing problem you could solve in a structured way.

Then build it properly.

You do not need to reinvent your company overnight. You need to identify the right priorities and align them with your three-year plan. This is about intentionally building your business, step by step, toward your long-term vision.

FREEDOM FACTORS

1. PREDICTABILITY BUILDS VALUE

Recurring revenue reduces uncertainty, and uncertainty is what buyers discount. The more visible and reliable your future cash flow, the more confidence your business commands.

2. RECURRING REVENUE IS EARNED THROUGH DELIVERY

It is not a billing trick. It requires systems, discipline, and consistent value. When customers stay month after month, it's because your business works and not because your contract is clever.

3. PREDICTABLE INCOME CREATES OPTIONS

When revenue compounds and churn is controlled, you gain space to invest, to step back, to scale, or to sell. Recurring revenue doesn't just increase valuation. It increases freedom

Part Four: Succession

Most books on succession planning focus on the exit itself: deal structures, negotiations, tax strategy, and the mechanics of getting to a close. That work matters. But it's not the focus here.

This section is about transition. The human, cultural, and leadership work required to hand a business forward without losing what made it worth building in the first place. It's about closing one chapter with intention and beginning the next with clarity.

Because succession is not just a transaction. It is a transfer of ownership, yes, but also of story, culture, and purpose. When those don't make the transition, the company may continue operating, but the essence of what made it special can quietly fade.

I am not trying to turn you into an M&A expert. There are excellent advisors and books that cover the mechanics. What I will do is walk you through the succession process in a way that applies regardless of the path you choose.

That path might be a traditional sale: to a strategic buyer, a private equity partner, or a management team. Or it might involve one of the employee ownership models gaining traction in values driven companies, such as ESOPs, Employee Ownership Trusts, worker cooperatives, or other purpose protecting structures designed to broaden ownership while preserving independence.

We will reference the mechanics where they matter. But the deeper aim is different: to help you make decisions aligned with your people, your purpose, and your legacy, and to prepare both your company and yourself so that when the time comes, you are not exhausted, cornered, or filled with regret.

Why Succession Matters Right Now

This conversation carries urgency, whether you plan to transition in twelve months or ten years, because three powerful forces are converging.

First, the Silver Tsunami. A significant wave of business owners is nearing transition at the same time. More companies will come to market. Buyers will become more selective. And many owners will discover, often too late, that optionality disappears when time pressure takes over.

Second, a shortage of ready leadership. Many companies lack a deep bench. Strong leaders are tough to find, harder to keep, and often stretched thin. Succession gets exponentially harder when the business is still overly dependent on the founder and the next generation of leadership isn't fully ready.

Third, economic uncertainty. Whether it's a slowdown, tighter capital, or a tough cycle, uncertain conditions compress timelines and reduce choices. The businesses that win in those moments are the ones that prepared early because preparation creates options.

That's why succession planning is no longer an end-of-game activity. It's a leadership responsibility, one that protects the people who helped you build the business, preserves the culture you fought to create, and gives you a real choice about what comes next.

You don't just want to exit. You want to **transition**.
You want to protect your people. You want the story to survive you.
You want the next chapter to be intentional, for the business *and* for yourself.

That's what we're going to do in the chapters that follow.

CHAPTER 16:
The Succession Challenge

"The biggest succession challenge is getting clear on what you really want—not just financially, but for your people, your purpose, and your legacy."

—Eric Rieger, Founder of WebIT

I remember the first time I began to think seriously about selling my business.

It was May 2013. I was sitting in a training room at ZingTrain (Zingerman's business education arm) in Ann Arbor, Michigan. Bo Burlingham was there, sharing early work from what would eventually become *Finish Big*.[43]

At the time, selling a company was barely part of the mainstream business conversation, certainly not to the extent it is today. Most discussions were dominated by the startup narrative: venture funding, hypergrowth, and hustle. There was far less attention on building enduring, bootstrapped companies, creating transferable value, or thinking seriously about life after an exit. That conversation began to shift as voices like John Warrillow and Burlingham brought value creation, succession, and stewardship into the open.

What struck me that day wasn't the idea of selling a business. It was Burlingham's focus on what *comes after*. Not the deal mechanics, but the emotional and psychological reality of leaving something you've poured yourself into. *Finish Big* wasn't about maximizing multiples. It was about identity, regret, and the challenge of finding purpose once the business is no longer yours.

That conversation planted a seed.

---

43   Bo Burlingham, *Finish Big: How Great Entrepreneurs Exit Their Companies on Top* (New York: Penguin Random House, 2014).

From Scarcity to Overload

Fast forward a decade, and according to the Exit Planning Institute, 70 percent of owners are now aware of their exit options.[44] But awareness is not the same as preparation. Only a third of family businesses have a documented and communicated succession plan. And perhaps the most telling, only 20 to 30 percent of businesses that go to market actually sell.

In many ways, the pendulum has swung too far in the opposite direction. We've gone from silence to saturation.

There are podcasts, courses, newsletters, masterminds, and LinkedIn influencers dedicated entirely to exits. Entire communities are built around acquiring businesses using seller financing or zero-money-down deals. Some of this work is thoughtful and legitimate. Much of it isn't.

The exit industry has started to resemble the startup scene of a decade ago—loud, crowded, and full of promises of "freedom" that often leave founders feeling pressured, confused, or worse, regretful.

What's missing in much of this conversation is the human side of succession the part Burlingham was pointing to all those years ago. About what it means to transfer not just ownership, but purpose. About how to prepare a company and yourself so that the transition strengthens what you built instead of hollowing it out.

Why This Matters

The end of a business journey is not just a financial event. It's a psychological shift, a human transition.

If you haven't done the inner work about what comes next, who you will be, how you will contribute, where your energy will go, you risk walking away with money, but without meaning.

---

44   The Exit Planning Institute, *2023 National State of Owner Readiness Report*, https://exit-planning-institute.org/state-of-owner-readiness, accessed January 2025.

Earlier in the book, we explored how a business can become the primary vessel for an entrepreneur's purpose. It provides rhythm to the day, meaning to decisions, and a community to serve. Over time, it doesn't just shape what you do, it shapes who you believe yourself to be.

That dynamic doesn't suddenly disappear at exit. It simply changes form.

When I interviewed Davin Salvagno on my podcast, he spoke about the idea that we each carry multiple expressions of purpose. We are parents, partners, friends, citizens, leaders, *and* business owners. The business is only one container for that purpose, even if it has been the dominant one for decades.[45]

The challenge is not that purpose vanishes when the company changes hands. It's that many entrepreneurs have allowed one expression of purpose to carry most of the weight. When that structure is removed or redefined, it can feel like the why itself has disappeared.

Take James Ashford.

He built GoProposal into a market-leading software company in five years and sold it to a FT100 firm for an eight-figure sum. No outside funding. No pedigree in the industry. Just grit, learning, and relentless focus.

From the outside, it was a dream outcome.

But when the deal closed, something unexpected happened. The structure that had defined his days disappeared. The urgency, the competition, the constant solving of problems. All gone.

As he later shared on Dominic Monkhouse's podcast:

"I sold the business and achieved all my reasons why. Done it. Ticked every single box. And then I fell off the cliff because I hadn't addressed the ultimate reason why entrepreneurs do what we do: we just love doing it. I love the grind, the fight, the

---

45   Moncrieff, "Episode 56: Thieves of Purpose." Accessed November 20 2025.

scrap, the learning. And when it was gone, I was literally on my hands and knees at the side of the road, thinking the world was coming to an end."[46]

It took counseling, therapy, and the guidance of mentors to help him build what he called the "scaffolding" for his second half—life beyond GoProposal.

Ashford's story is dramatic, but it isn't rare. When your business has been the primary vessel for meaning—your structure, your identity, your community—an exit can feel less like a finish line and more like a free fall.

Paul Spiegelman's journey was different.

When Spiegelman built Beryl Health, he was intentional from early on about culture, purpose, and long-term thinking. When offers first came from private equity, he did not rush. In fact, he walked away from an early deal because he felt it would compromise the culture he had built.

Instead, he reinvested.

He put money back into the business. He strengthened the leadership team. He invested in technology. He doubled down on the model he believed in. Only later, when a determined buyer who valued the culture Spiegelman and his team had built, did he choose to sell.

And even then, he had already been thinking about what came next.

Before the sale, he had started the Small Giants Community. He had been writing and speaking. Building a sense of purpose beyond Beryl. When he joined Stericycle as chief culture officer, it was by choice. An experiment. A new chapter.

Spiegelman did not react to an exit. He was intentional about shaping his transition.

---

46   Monkhouse, D, 'Episode 311: The Importance of Creating Amazing Customer Experiences with James Ashford', *Curious Leadership with Dominic Monkhouse* (2024), https://podcasts.apple.com/ca/podcast/e311-the-importance-of-creating-amazing/ id13982128891?i=1000666001550 accessed 22 November 2025

As he told me in our conversation, the search for purpose never ends. It evolves. It shifts. But it does not disappear.[47]

That brings us back to something we covered earlier in the book.

For many entrepreneurs, the business becomes the primary vessel for purpose. It gives structure to the day. Meaning to decisions. A community to serve. It shapes identity.

But the mistake we make is to over index on one purpose. As Davin Salvagno pointed out, when I interviewed him on *The Freedom Experience* podcast. We carry many purposes in life. We have a purpose as a parent, as a partner, as a friend, as a community leader.

The danger is not losing our purpose, it's over investing in one expression of it.

If the business becomes the only arena where meaning lives, then any transition will feel destabilizing. Not because purpose is gone, but because it has not been diversified.

There is growing research that helps explain this dynamic.

Entrepreneurial identity is powerful.[48] It fuels resilience, creativity, and perseverance. But when too much of your self worth becomes tied to one role, the loss of that role can feel like a loss of self.

Studies on social identity show that when founders anchor their identity almost entirely in the business, an exit can destabilize more than income.[49] It can unsettle structure, status, community, and meaning all at once.

---

47   Jean Moncrieff, "Episode 27: Culture as Strategy: How Purpose and Values Drove a 22X Valuation with Paul Spiegelman," *The Freedom Experience with Jean Moncrieff* (2024), https://www.jeanmoncrieff.com/podcasts/the-freedom-experience-with-jean-moncrieff/episodes/2148894952 accessed November 15, 2024.

48   Hongtao Yang, Lei Zhang, Yenchun Jim Wu, and Hangyu Shi, "Benefits and Costs of Happy Entrepreneurs: The Dual Effect of Entrepreneurial Identity on Entrepreneurs" Subjective Well-Being," *Frontiers in Psychology*, 12 (2021), https://doi.org/10.3389/fpsyg.2021.767164.

49   Estelle Fauchart and Marc Gruber, "Entrepreneurial Identity: Strategic Identity and Firm Behavior," *Academy of Management Journal* 54, no.5 (2011); 935–957, https://doi.org/10.5465/amj.2009.0881.

Without other well-developed anchors in life, the transition can bring disorientation, regret, or burnout.

That is why some owners achieve an exceptional financial outcome and still feel hollow.

Succession is not just about getting out.

It is about getting out intact—financially, emotionally, and spiritually.

I Thought I Was Ready

Subconsciously, I'd probably been thinking about selling my business for a while and Burlington's book brought those thoughts to the surface and set the wheels in motion.

South Africa was in a difficult place. Crime was a constant challenge. Corruption was widespread. Basic infrastructure beginning to crumble. I was worried about the future of the country, and even more worried about my children's future.

So, I made what felt like a rational decision. It was time to sell the business.

At the same time, an opportunity was opening in the United States. I found myself commuting between South Africa and Denver, trying to run the business, negotiate a sale, and imagine what life might look like on the other side. It was exhausting, but it also felt energizing. My *why* as an entrepreneur, husband, and father was shifting.

Freedom, adventure, curiosity, and independence had always mattered to me. Those values had been shaped during my time in 1980s America, and I felt a deep pull back toward that version of myself and that way of life.

I thought I had it all worked out. Sell the companies in South Africa and use the proceeds to establish a new business in the United States. At the time, the South African currency was still strong against the US dollar.

In reality, my business was not in a position to sell. My already fragile marriage wasn't strong enough to survive a relocation to another country. And if I am honest, I was the deeper issue. The business was unstable, but so was I.

The best offer that came across the table included a five- to six-year earn out. It was a nonstarter. I was already burned out and emotionally drained. I did not want to keep traveling. I did not want to stay tied to the business. I wanted to be present with my family and put all my focus into the next chapter.

At the time, I told myself the offer was unreasonable. How could they expect me to stay involved for another five years?

Looking back, the truth was harder to admit. Neither the business nor I were ready.

I had not built a company that could thrive without me. I had not created enough leadership depth. Too much of the operational weight still ran through my hands. And I had never seriously imagined a future that did not revolve around being the founder and CEO.

What I believed was a successful company looked very different through the eyes of an acquirer.

And more importantly, I hadn't done the inner work of transition. I knew what I wanted to leave *behind*. I had very little clarity about what I was moving *toward*.

More importantly, I had not done the inner work of transition. I knew what I wanted to leave behind, but I had very little clarity about what I was moving toward. The move to the U.S. was driven more by emotion than intention. I was hitting the eject button on both my business and my country, relocating my young family to a place that had shaped my early life, yet held little personal connection for my them.

That gap, the space between "I'm done with this" and having thoughtfully considered what comes next, is where many succession stories begin to unravel. Not because the business lacks value, but because the founder has not yet been intentional about what they are moving toward.

In my case, there was no real clarity about what I was going to build in the U.S. There was an opportunity to invest in something new, but I had never properly explored it. I treated it like a parachute. Something to give me a soft landing, rather than something I had deliberately chosen.

It turned out that parachute was riddled with holes.

What followed was not a clean transition into a new chapter. Over the next few years, the strain contributed to the breakdown of my marriage and a period in my life where I drifted into unhealthy patterns, including drinking too much and losing direction.

That is the danger of leaving without truly deciding where you are going.

The Silver Tsunami

What I went through was not unusual. It was simply early.

I was forced to confront succession before my business was ready and before I had done the personal work required to step away. I had to rebuild under pressure. Many owners will not have that luxury.

Today, millions of business owners are approaching the same crossroads. This is what people call the Silver Tsunami—a generational wave of ownership transition that is already reshaping the private business landscape. However you measure it, the direction is clear: a significant portion of privately held companies will change hands in the coming decade.

And when supply increases, buyers gain leverage.

As more businesses come to market at the same time, capital becomes selective. Valuations compress. Deal terms tighten. Buyers can afford to be selective. Owners who have not prepared early often discover something uncomfortable: optionality disappears when urgency arrives.

But the real pressure is not only financial. It is structural and personal.

Many owners still sit at the center of everything. Key decisions live in their heads. Customer relationships run through them. Leadership depth is thin. Systems are poorly developed and incomplete. And identity is still tightly tied to the role of the owner.

Succession and transition planning can no longer sit on the "someday" list. It is part of responsible leadership. The founders who navigate it well are usually the ones who begin preparing while they still have time and flexibility.

Early preparation expands your range of choices. And having real choices allows you to decide what kind of transition makes sense for you, your people, and your company.

Alternative Paths to Succession

When a wave of owners hits the market at once, the default advice becomes dangerously simple: *sell to the highest bidder while you still can.*

But for many founders, especially those who've built businesses with deep relationships, strong cultures, and real community roots, that advice doesn't feel like freedom. It feels like walking away from something you love. Something you have poured years into shaping. An entity you want to see continue to grow, evolve, and thrive long after you step aside.

On the other hand, the acquirer isn't always buying what you care about most.

They're buying cash flow, customer concentration, and operational leverage. They're buying a platform. And in too many cases, the very things that made the business special—the way you treat people, the standards you've protected, the founding story that shaped your culture—become "soft" assets that get stripped away in the name of value creation or optimization.

That's why alternative succession paths matter. They aren't just trendy structures or clever financial engineering. They're responses to a real, emotional problem:

How do you transition ownership without losing the soul of the company?

In the Small Giants Community, I've noticed something encouraging. More owners are looking beyond the traditional binary choice of "sell or shut down" and exploring models that allow the business to continue *as itself*—not as a diluted version of what a buyer wants it to become.

We're seeing more employee ownership—through Employee Stock Ownership Plans (ESOPs), Employee Ownership Trusts (EOTs), Worker Co-Operatives, and some creative hybrid approaches. We're seeing founders design "DIY" transitions that fit their company's size, economics, and culture. We're seeing purpose-driven structures that protect mission over time, not just value at close.

What unites these owners isn't ideology. It's conviction.

They want a transition that protects:

- **Their people** (the ones who built it with them)
- **Their culture** (the behaviors and standards that make it work)
- **Their community** (the place that shaped the business and depends on it)
- **Their founding story** (the purpose that explains why the business exists in the first place)

And that conviction makes sense when you consider what values-driven companies tend to share:

- **Intimacy with staff.** These founders know their people by name. They've lived through hard seasons together. "Success" isn't measured only in EBITDA—it's measured in livelihoods.

- **Resistance to the status quo.** These businesses didn't follow the standard playbook to grow. So, it's no surprise they're refusing to follow the standard playbook to transition.

- **Deep community ties.** These companies aren't just located in a community—they're woven into it. When they disappear, something real is lost.

When businesses close, or sell to outsiders who don't share their DNA, employees lose stability, customers lose trust, and communities lose anchors. And founders often lose something too: the satisfaction of knowing the thing they built will still mean something after they step away.

That's what these alternative paths protect.

They allow you to transition without selling off what matters most, so the founding story doesn't vanish the moment the paperwork is signed.

BEYOND THE HIGHEST BIDDER

When succession becomes real, many founders are told the same thing: maximize the valuation and sell while the timing is right.

That advice is not wrong. But it is incomplete.

For founders who have built companies rooted in purpose, culture, and community, the highest bidder is not always the best successor. A buyer may pay well for the cash flow while having little interest in the values that shaped it.

John Abrams chose a different path.

In the late 1980s, long before employee ownership became fashionable, Abrams began asking a question most founders postpone:

What happens to this company when I am no longer here to hold it together?

South Mountain Company, his design and building firm on Martha's Vineyard, was successful and respected. He could have kept it tightly held. He could have sold at a later date. Instead, he began designing for continuity early.

It wasn't a simple decision. Abrams has spoken openly about the fear involved in loosening his grip. The business was not just an asset. It was something he loved:

"My fear was that this thing that we had created, that I loved, I would end up not loving once I lost control. Well, that never happened. It only got better." [50]

That statement captures the heart of alternative succession model.

By distributing ownership and responsibility, Abrams ensured that purpose was not trapped inside the founder. It was embedded in the culture, in the structure, and in the people.

When he retired in 2022, South Mountain did not falter. It continued, rooted in its community and guided by the same values that shaped it decades earlier.

Abrams did not simply exit well. He transitioned well.

He built a company where purpose could outlive him.

That is what lies beyond the highest bidder: not just a transaction, but continuity. Not just value at close, but values carried forward.

The Transition of Purpose

Most books talk about succession in terms of ownership and valuation. But the hardest transition for a founder isn't handing over the keys and banking the check.

It's letting go of their *why*.

---

50   Jean Moncrieff, "Episode 43: Why Business Owners Should Rethink Ownership with John Abrams," *The Freedom Experience with Jean Moncrieff* (2025), https://podcasts. apple.com/ca/podcast/episode-43-why-business-owners-should-rethink-ownership/ id1485708333 accessed November 20, 2025.

For years, the business has been the primary vessel for purpose. It is where creativity, ambition, impact, and identity converge. It gives structure to the day and meaning to decisions. When that vessel changes or disappears, we don't just lose a role. We lose rhythm, momentum, and our why.

That is why even well executed exits can feel disorienting.

James Ashford's experience was not a failure of success; he had a wildly successful exit. Rather, it was a failure of transition. The business had been carrying most of his sense of purpose. When it was gone, nothing had been intentionally built to take its place.

John Abrams took a different path. By embedding ownership and shared governance into South Mountain Company early, he ensured that purpose did not live inside him alone. It was distributed into the structure, the culture, and the people. When he stepped back, the purpose did not vanish. It evolved.

That is what I mean by a Transition of Purpose.

It is the work of carrying meaning forward from one chapter into the next. Not replacing your purpose, but re-expressing it.

The expression may change:

- From builder to mentor
- From operator to steward
- From being at the center to developing others
- From running a company to shaping people, ideas, or communities

Without that transition, succession feels abrupt. You leave the business, but you do not arrive anywhere new.

I have felt this outside of business. When my daughter left for university in Italy, I drove away feeling anxious for her, proud of her, and unexpectedly empty. My role as a father had not ended, but my why had shifted. The purpose remained. The expression changed.

The mistake many founders make is assuming this evolution will sort itself out after the exit. It will not. Like strategy, culture, or leadership, it requires intention.

And here is the deeper insight: how you design succession inside the business shapes how you experience transition outside of it. When purpose is shared and embedded, you can step back without feeling erased.

FREEDOM FACTORS

1. SEPARATE YOUR IDENTITY FROM YOUR ROLE

Your business may be a powerful vessel for purpose, but it is not the only one. Build other anchors before you need them.

2. DESIGN FOR CONTINUITY, NOT JUST EXIT

When purpose is embedded in culture, structure, and shared ownership, it can outlive the founder. That makes transition healthier for everyone.

3. BE INTENTIONAL ABOUT YOUR NEXT EXPRESSION

Do not wait until after the deal closes to ask who you are becoming. Succession is not only about leaving well. It is about arriving well.

CHAPTER 17:
Clarify Your Number, and Your Why

Some business owners lean heavily toward purpose and neglect the math. They care deeply about their people, their culture, and the legacy they want to leave behind, but they have never clearly defined what they need financially to step away with confidence. They assume it will work itself out because the mission feels strong.

Others lean in the opposite direction. They track valuation, watch market multiples, and negotiate hard when opportunity appears. But they never slow down to define what they're walking toward. They can protect their balance sheet and still find themselves adrift once the deal closes.

In reality, most owners aren't one or the other. We care about both. We want to do right by our people and our community, and we also want financial security for ourselves and our families. The risk isn't choosing the wrong side. The risk is failing to align the two by treating purpose and economics as separate conversations, when they are two parts of the same decision.

You can structure a deal that protects employees and still lose your own sense of direction. You can maximize financial outcome and still feel unsettled about what comes next. Succession becomes fragile when purpose and economics are treated as separate conversations instead of two parts of the same decision.

You have already done the hard work of building something meaningful. This chapter is about bringing that same level of intention to your transition. It is about clarifying what kind of life you are building toward and understanding what the business must deliver to make that life viable. Until those two are aligned, any exit conversation is incomplete.

TWO VERY DIFFERENT OUTCOMES

Bruce Eckfeldt remembers the realization that he had outgrown his business.

He had built a successful design and architecture firm in New York City. The company had a good client base and steady momentum. Nothing was broken. But over time, the work stopped energizing him. The curiosity that once drove him began to fade.

"I probably stayed three years too long," he told me.

The business hadn't failed him. He had simply evolved beyond the role he once loved. But without clarity about what came next, letting go felt risky. His identity was still tied to being the founder, the expert, the one people relied on.

By the time Eckfeldt sold, he was depleted. The exit brought relief, but it confirmed something important: when purpose and timing drift apart, succession happens on the business's terms, not yours.

Carl Erickson approached the question differently.

From early on, Erickson embedded values like *Give a Shit* and *Own It* into Atomic Object's culture. Over time, those values shaped how decisions were made, how people were hired, and how ownership was distributed. The business was never just about revenue. It was about stewardship.

When Erickson began thinking about stepping back, the conversation didn't begin with valuation. It began with continuity. What would protect the culture? How could leadership expand rather than contract? How could ownership reflect the contribution of the people who had built the company?

Atomic transitioned to broad employee ownership. Leadership responsibilities were shared. Wealth creation was shared. Erickson reduced his involvement gradually and ultimately exited on terms aligned with what he valued.

He didn't step away from his purpose. He redirected it.

The difference between Eckfeldt and Erickson isn't intelligence or ambition. It's alignment.

Eckfeldt stayed longer than he should have because he hadn't defined what came next. Erickson prepared early and built a structure that allowed him to step back without destabilizing what he had created.

What's Your Number?

When I talk to business owners about succession, I often ask a simple question:

What's your number?

Not the valuation you *hope* for. Not the number your buddy got when he sold. Not the headline figure you see thrown around in your industry. I mean the real number. The amount of after-tax cash you need to fund the next chapter of your life with confidence.

Most owners don't know it, and it's not because they're careless. It's because the "exit industry" rarely teaches people to separate three very different numbers:

- **The sale price**
  (what someone might pay)
- **The net proceeds**
  (what you keep after taxes, fees, and deal structure)
- **The lifestyle number**
  (what you actually need to live the life you want)

Until you run that math, you're negotiating in the dark, reacting to offers and multiples without knowing whether the outcome truly serves you.

This is also where owners can get pulled into a vanity trap. Chasing an impressive multiple. Pushing for the bigger headline. Staying longer than they want because the next turn of the crank might raise the valuation. The tragedy is that many founders aren't chasing "enough." They're chasing an undefined finish line, and undefined finish lines have a way of keeping you stuck.

Your number is personal. It depends on the life you want to live, the people you're responsible for, how long you expect those funds to last, and the realities of taxes, risk, and inflation. For one owner, that might mean $2 million because you're moving onto something new and exciting and need seed capital. For another, it might be $20 million because you're retiring. The point isn't the number, it's the alignment between the number and what comes next.

Everybody Has Their Number

Take Gary Erickson and Kit Crawford at Clif Bar—one of the original companies Bo Burlingham profiled in Small Giants.[51] In 2000, Erickson famously walked away from a **$120 million offer from Quaker Oats** because it didn't align with how they wanted to grow and steward the business. That choice wasn't about stubbornness; it was about purpose. They believed Clif Bar could be a different kind of company focused on people, sustainability, and community, not just profit.

A decade later, Clif Bar created an **Employee Stock Ownership Plan (ESOP)**, giving employees a meaningful ownership stake in the business. Then in **2022**, they agreed to sell Clif Bar to Mondelēz International in a deal reported at about **$2.9 billion**—an outcome that created a substantial financial result for the founders *and* benefited employee-owners through the ESOP.

---

51   Burlingham, B, *Small Giants: Companies That Choose to Be Great Instead of Big* (Portfolio, 2016)

But the story doesn't end at a payday.

After stepping back from day-to-day leadership years before the sale, Erickson didn't retreat into retirement. Instead, he has continued to live a purpose-driven life, staying connected to community, sustainability, and entrepreneurship. He has taken part in forums, podcasts, and broader conversations about purpose driven business, including interviews on platforms such as *How I Built This* with Guy Raz, where he reflects on leadership, values, and what it takes to build companies that endure beyond a transaction.

In Clif Bar's case, the **number aligned with the why and with the people** because Erickson and Crawford didn't treat succession as a financial exit alone. They created a structure where the business could continue to serve its employees and its mission, and they walked into the next chapter having planned that part of their lives with intention.

ALIGNING PURPOSE AND NUMBERS

Erickson's story works because it exposes a common myth: purpose and money sit on opposite ends of the table.

They don't.

What matters isn't maximizing one at the expense of the other, it's alignment.

When Erickson and Crawford turned down the Quaker Oats offer, they weren't rejecting money. They were rejecting a future that didn't fit their values. When they later created an ESOP, they weren't giving up upside, they were widening who benefited from it. And when they eventually sold Clif Bar, they did so in a way that honored the people and the mission that made the business valuable in the first place.

That's what alignment can look like at scale.

But you don't need a billion-dollar outcome to live this principle.

Earlier in the book, we met Eric Rieger, founder of WEBIT Services. Rieger's purpose isn't abstract. It shows up in the choices he's making, especially as succession gets closer. While private equity firms continue to approach him with lucrative offers, Eric has chosen a different path: transitioning WEBIT to **100 percent employee ownership by 2030**.

He knows it may not deliver the biggest personal payout. But it aligns with what matters most to him: *closing the wealth gap*.

Erickson's story and Rieger's story aren't the same. But the pattern is.

Your *why* defines what matters.
Your *number* defines what's required.

When those two are in conflict, succession becomes difficult. You hesitate. You second-guess. You stay too long or rush too fast. When they're aligned, decisions simplify, even when the decision itself is hard.

Sometimes alignment means accepting a lower valuation in exchange for protecting culture or rewarding employees. Sometimes it means staying involved longer to steward the transition. And sometimes it means choosing a traditional exit because it best supports your next chapter *and* the future of the business.

The key is intention.

For founders like Rieger and Erickson, the "best" exit isn't the one with the biggest headline (although Erickson certainly found his number). It's the one that lets you step forward knowing you did the best to look after your people, fulfill your purpose, and that your next chapter is funded and meaningful.

That's why succession planning can't start with a spreadsheet. It must start with clarity.

When purpose and numbers are aligned, succession stops being a trade-off. It becomes a continuation.

The Stewardship Shift

If succession is the challenge, stewardship is the mindset shift that makes it possible.

Most founders never fully make the leap from owner-operator to true owner. They stay central, approving, solving, rescuing, and holding the business together through force of will. The company may grow, but it remains dependent. And when the succession question finally arrives, it doesn't feel like a transition. It feels like an emergency.

Stewardship is different.

Stewardship is the decision to treat the business as something you're responsible for, and not something you're trapped inside. It's recognizing that you're not just building value for a potential buyer. You're shaping and nurturing an organization that endures well beyond your tenure.

That shift protects what matters most in a values-driven business:

- **Your people**—the team whose livelihoods and pride are tied to the company
- **Your purpose**—the founding story and standards that guide decisions
- **Your culture**—the "how we do things here" that customers feel and employees live
- **Your community**—the relationships and reputation that took years to earn

And it changes how you think about succession.

Instead of asking only, *"What can I get for this business?"* stewardship asks: "What needs to be true for this business to thrive without me?"

That question leads to very practical work:

- reducing dependence on the founder
- strengthening the leadership bench

- documenting what lives in people's heads
- building systems that make excellence repeatable
- creating governance that protects what you don't want lost

This is where the earlier work in the book matters. The shift from operator to owner. The focus on building a leadership team that can carry the business forward. The move from "growth at all costs" to intentional growth rooted in purpose.

Succession is simply the moment those choices get tested.

If you've already begun living as a steward, succession becomes a set of options. If you haven't, succession becomes a scramble.

And here's the paradox: stewardship doesn't reduce your freedom, it increases it. The more your business can run without you, the more choices you have: to sell, to transition to employees, to step back into a chair role, to stay involved as a mentor, to design your next chapter without panic.

Stewardship is what turns succession from an event into a transition.

Emotional Readiness: Preparing for the Shift

Even when the strategy is clear and the numbers make sense, succession can still feel unsettling.

That's because transitioning out of a business is not just a financial calculation. It is a leadership decision that reshapes your role, your influence, and your daily rhythm. And those shifts are rarely neutral.

On paper, everything can look ready. The valuation works. The leadership team is capable. The structure is sound. Yet something inside hesitates. That hesitation is not weakness. It is information.

In my experience, founders often move through a quiet emotional sequence as succession becomes real. At first, there is excitement. Freedom. Possibility. The idea of new space in your calendar and new chapters ahead.

Then comes doubt. Questions surface. Is this the right time? What happens to my people? Will I regret stepping back?

Sometimes there is grief, even when the outcome is strong. The business has been central to your life for decades. It has structured your days and sharpened your decisions. Letting go of that role is not nothing.

None of these reactions mean you shouldn't move forward. They mean you're human.

Burlingham wrote in *Finish Big* that leaving a company is often harder than building one. The founders who struggle most are not the least successful. They are the ones who underestimated the emotional weight of transition.

Emotional readiness does not mean you eliminate uncertainty. It means you acknowledge it before it drives your decisions.

When purpose is clear and your number is defined, emotional readiness becomes the final alignment check. Not a barrier—but a safeguard.

THE THREE DIMENSIONS OF EXIT READINESS

When owners say they are "ready," they usually mean financially ready. The valuation works. The market is favorable. The advisors are in place.

But real readiness has three dimensions, and weakness in any one of them will show up under pressure.

The first is purpose. Without clarity about what you are moving toward, every offer feels either too small or too risky. You hesitate not because the deal is wrong, but because the direction is unclear.

The second is emotional readiness. Even with alignment on paper, hesitation can surface. Doubt, attachment, fear of regret... these are not signs of failure. They are signals. Ignoring them doesn't make them disappear; it simply allows them to influence decisions unconsciously.

The third is financial clarity. This is your anchor. Not the headline valuation, but the after-tax reality. Not the sale price, but the number required to fund the life you intend to live. Without that clarity, you are negotiating against emotion and market noise rather than your own definition of enough.

When these three are aligned, succession becomes navigable. When one is missing, business owners fumble, rush, or second-guess themselves at critical moments.

Every path that follows—strategic sale, private equity, management buyout, employee ownership—will test these three dimensions simultaneously. Alignment here makes the mechanics simpler later.

Crafting Your Timeline

One of the most common succession mistakes is underestimating how long preparation takes.

Not the transaction. The preparation.

Succession is not a moment. It is a design process. And the earlier that process begins, the more deliberate your choices become.

Think of your timeline as a runway. A short runway forces acceleration and risk. A long runway gives you lift.

THREE-PLUS YEARS OUT: LAYING THE GROUNDWORK

At this stage, you are not selling the business. You are strengthening it.

This is where earlier decisions about leadership, systems, and stewardship are either validated or exposed. You clarify long-term intent. You deepen leadership capacity. You reduce single points of failure, especially yourself. You ensure the financial story is clean and credible.

Whether or not you ever sell, this work increases resilience. It creates optionality before you need it.

TWO YEARS OUT: BUILDING READINESS

Now the focus shifts from strengthening to preparing.

You assemble advisors. You formalize documentation. You sharpen your growth narrative. You pressure-test leadership depth.

More importantly, you pressure-test yourself. Are you willing to release control? Can the company perform without your daily intervention? If the answers are unclear, that is information. And information at this stage is valuable.

ONE YEAR OUT: CREATING OPTIONS

By this stage, you're not locked into a decision. You're creating *choices*.

You might begin quiet conversations with potential buyers. Or explore employee ownership structures. Or formalize a management succession plan. The point isn't to rush, it's to explore what's possible.

Founders who start early get to compare paths. Founders who wait often get presented with only one.

WHY PLANNING EARLY MATTERS

Planning early isn't about surrendering control. It is about shaping the transition before urgency shapes it for you.

Time increases leverage—not just financial leverage, but cultural and structural leverage. It allows you to protect what matters, reward the right people, and structure a transition that reflects your values rather than reacting to external pressure.

And even if you decide not to exit for years, the preparation improves the overall business health. Leadership becomes stronger. Strategy becomes clearer. The weight on your shoulders becomes lighter.

Succession planning, done well, does not pull you toward the end. It strengthens the business now and gives you the freedom to decide later.

FREEDOM FACTORS

1. ALIGNMENT SIMPLIFIES HARD DECISIONS

When your purpose is clear and your number is defined, succession stops feeling like a gamble. Clarity removes ego, noise, and pressure from the decision.

2. READINESS IS MULTIDIMENSIONAL

True exit readiness requires alignment across purpose, emotional readiness, and financial clarity. Weakness in any one of them will surface under pressure.

3. TIME CREATES OPTIONALITY

Succession is designed, not declared. The earlier you strengthen leadership, reduce dependency, and clarify intent, the more choices you preserve.

CHAPTER 18:
The Evolving Exit Landscape

In the last two chapters, we looked inward. We explored the Transition of Purpose, arguably the hardest part of succession, when you hand off not just ownership but your *why*. We also clarified your number, grounding financial reality in personal intent.

Now it's time to look outward.

Once you know what matters most to you, the question becomes: **how do you design a transition that reflects it?**

This is where many founders stumble. They know they don't want to sell to the highest bidder, but they're unclear about what real alternatives exist. The good news is that the succession landscape has evolved. More owners are exploring ownership models that broaden participation, preserve culture, and carry purpose forward, putting employees in the ownership seat rather than handing the company to the market alone.

When "Mojo" Disappears

We all know the story.

A beloved regional company, admired in its community for decades, sells to a larger firm. Overnight, the energy shifts. Decisions move from the office down the hall to a distant headquarters. Long-time employees leave. Customers feel it.

What was once a thriving part of the community becoming just another logo under a corporate umbrella.

Financially, the transaction may be a win for the owner. But the company's mojo—that business equivalent of charisma—it likely eroded.

When I interviewed Dr. Greg Toback, he shared how, as a student pharmacist in the late 1980s, he worked in an independent pharmacy on Long Island. One night, an older pharmacist pulled him aside and said, *"Pharmacy is changing fast. One day this place will be owned by a national chain."*[52] At the time, it sounded ridiculous. Years later, Toback watched that prediction come true as pharmacy consolidated into big brands and the local model disappeared.

Toback later became a dentist, and years after that comment, he saw the same consolidation pattern emerging again in dentistry. Practices were being bought up by larger groups, decisions moved away from the practitioner, and more layers were inserted between the doctor and the patient.

Sure, it makes sense financially: bigger networks, more resources, professional management. But the real impact shows up downstream. As more layers enter the system the relationships at the heart of the business becomes harder to protect. In dentistry, that relationship is the bond between doctor and patient. In your company, it's the bond between your people and your customers.

Toback also pointed to a second-order effect most owners don't see until it's too late: consolidation can lock out the next generation. When large buyers bid up valuations, young professionals—already burdened by student debt—can't afford to buy in. So, the industry becomes less entrepreneurial, less personal, and less resilient over time.

This is why so many business owners are exploring alternatives. They're not just asking *how much* they can get, but more conscious of what's being eroded in the process.

---

52   Jean Moncrieff, Episode 67, "Why Business Owners are Rethinking Ownership with Peter Koehler," *The Freedom Experience with Jean Moncrieff,* https://youtu.be/ks7LenSgj8g?si=_EGKPYqzV5SOFixF, accessed January 7, 2026.

The Evergreen Company

Many owners exploring employee ownership aren't simply looking for a transition model. They're thinking longer term. They want to build a company that outlives them, one where the purpose is protected and the business continues to serve something larger than a transaction.

Dave Whorton describes this in his book *Another Way* and through the Tugboat Institute: companies designed to endure beyond the founder carry the founding story forward and resist being absorbed by an acquisition that doesn't fit.[53] These businesses aren't built for an exit. They're built for continuity.

At the heart of this approach is stewardship. Preserving what made the company distinctive. Passing on the narrative, not just the numbers. Creating enough structural protection that the business doesn't drift—slowly or suddenly—away from its original intent.

What follows isn't a menu of theoretical options. It's a set of real examples showing how values-driven founders are navigating ownership with intention, using different tools, making different trade-offs, and all wrestling with the same question:

How do I step back without watching what I built get hollowed out?

TEXT-EM-ALL: AN EMPLOYEE OWNERSHIP TRUST AS AN EVERGREEN ALTERNATIVE

For Brad Herrmann and Hai Nguyen, co-founders of Text-Em-All, the goal was never to build another SaaS company and flip it at the first attractive offer. From the start, they were building something more personal: a tech business grounded in people, values, and long-term stewardship.

---

53   Dave Wharton, *Another Way: Building Companies That Last...and Last...and Last*
     (Boston: Harvard Business Review Press, 2025).

Two decades later, with a thriving team and an enviable company culture, they began asking: *how do we ensure what we've built will last another 100 years?*

They explored options. A direct sale offered liquidity, but it also introduced the risk that decisions would move further away from the culture that had made the company work. They looked at employee ownership models, including an ESOP, and weighed the complexity and the unintended dynamics that can creep in when ownership becomes uneven or difficult to understand.

Eventually, they landed on an **Employee Ownership Trust (EOT)**—not as a trendy structure, and not as an "exit," but as an Evergreen move. A way to protect independence, keep the company aligned to its founding intent, and ensure that the value created over nearly two decades would be shared broadly with the people who helped build it.

In October 2023, Text-Em-All became the first 100 percent employee-owned SaaS company in the United States through an EOT. Today, trustees steward the company's mission, profits are shared inclusively, and employees know they're not just working *for* the company—they're building a legacy *within* it.

Brad summed it up in a way that fits the Small Giants ethos perfectly:

"We're not just introducing a new model; we're redefining success for business owners. By embracing shared ownership, we empower every team member."[54]

WHEN OWNERSHIP BECOMES A WAY OF THINKING: SRC AND THE ESOP MODEL

If Text-Em-All shows what Evergreen ownership looks like in a modern SaaS company, **SRC Holdings** proves this way of thinking can endure for decades.

---

54   Common Trust, "Text-Em-All: Employee Ownership Trust Case Study," *Common Trust*, https://www.common-trust.com/case-studies/text-em-all-employee-ownership-trust, accessed January 7, 2026.

In the early 1980s, Jack Stack and twelve managers took an audacious risk. They bought a failing International Harvester plant in Springfield, Missouri, putting down $100,000 and borrowing nearly $9 million. The odds were stacked against them. Most observers assumed they wouldn't survive.

Instead, they built one of the most celebrated employee-owned companies in the world.

The structure was an **Employee Stock Ownership Plan (ESOP)**, but the real innovation wasn't legal. It was cultural. Stack believed that ownership only mattered if people understood the business well enough to act like owners. So, he introduced **open-book management**, teaching every employee—from machinists to management—how the company actually made money, where it lost money, and how their decisions affected the whole system.

Over the next four decades, SRC grew into a group of companies whose value increased by more than 292,000 percent.[55] But the more important outcome wasn't financial. Employees didn't just share in equity; they shared in responsibility, decision-making, and pride.

Stack often said that ownership isn't a piece of paper—it's a way of thinking. At SRC, the ESOP wasn't an exit strategy. It was a commitment to build a business that could sustain itself without depending on a single founder.

That's the Evergreen lesson here. ESOPs can be powerful tools for long-term stewardship, but only when they're paired with a culture that treats transparency, education, and accountability as non-negotiable. Without that, employee ownership becomes symbolic. With it, it becomes transformative.

SRC's story shows that Evergreen ownership isn't fragile or idealistic. Done well, it's resilient. It can last generations. And it can turn a struggling

---

55   Rob Dube, "Winning the Game: Jack Stack on Why People Is the New Critical Number," *Forbes* (27 November 2018), https://www.forbes.com/sites/robdube/2018/11/27/winning-the-game-jack-stack-on-why-people-is-the-new-critical-number/, accessed January 7, 2026.

company into something far more valuable than a one-time transaction ever could.

STEWARDSHIP THROUGH TRUSTS

For some founders, shared ownership is only part of the answer. The deeper concern is how to lock in purpose and independence long after they step aside.

This is where trust-based structures (particularly Perpetual Purpose Trusts) are gaining traction. Rather than optimizing for a future sale, these structures are designed to steward a company's mission across generations. Governance can be customized. Values can be protected. And the business can be shielded from acquisitions that don't align with its founding intent.

When I spoke with Peter Koehler, he put it simply: purpose needs a vehicle.[56] Without structural protection, even the strongest values can erode once the founder is no longer in the room. Trusts provide that vehicle, not by freezing a business in time, but by setting clear guardrails around what must endure.

What's striking is that this isn't happening in isolation. At gatherings like **Stewards Circle**, founders and leaders from a wide range of industries are comparing notes on employee ownership and trust-based models. Not as clever exit strategies, but as long-term commitments to people, culture, and community. What connects them is a shared belief that ownership is an ongoing responsibility, not a finish line.

One of the original Small Giants, Zingerman's Community of Businesses, has taken this path as well. Rather than positioning the company for a conventional sale, Zingerman's adopted a Perpetual Purpose Trust to formally protect its independence and mission. The trust ensures the

---

56   Jean Moncrieff, "Episode 40, Why Business Owners are Rethinking Ownership with Peter Koehler," *The Freedom Experience with Jean Moncrieff*, https://youtu.be/ ks7LenSgj8g?si=_EGKPYqzV5S0FixF, accessed January 7, 2026.

business cannot be sold, franchised, or redirected away from the values and community focus that defined it from the beginning.

This wasn't a sudden move. It was the culmination of decades of intentional culture-building that ultimately translated into a legal structure designed to carry that intent forward.

Trusts aren't for everyone. They require patience, clarity, and a willingness to trade maximum liquidity for long-term stewardship. But for founders who care deeply about preserving their story, protecting their people, and keeping the company anchored to its purpose, they offer a powerful alternative.

In the context of succession, trust-based ownership shifts the question from *"Who will buy this business?"* to *"Who will be entrusted to carry it forward?"*

Other Paths: Designing Ownership to Fit the Business

Not every business owner chooses an ESOP, a trust, or a formal employee ownership plan. For some, the right answer is more bespoke, a structure designed to fit the size, culture, and values of the business rather than a predefined structure.

What unites these approaches isn't the legal form. It's the intent behind them: to create continuity, reward contribution, and ensure the business can thrive without being sold to a buyer who doesn't understand its story.

SOUTH MOUNTAIN COMPANY: A WORKER COOPERATIVE

On Martha's Vineyard, Abrams faced the same question many founders eventually confront: *what happens to this company when I step away?*

Rather than sell, Abrams transformed South Mountain Company into a worker cooperative. Ownership is shared among employee-owners who buy into the co-op, and governance follows a simple principle: one person, one vote.

This wasn't about maximizing payout. It was about aligning ownership with values—equity, community, and long-term sustainability. The structure created a culture where responsibility and reward were shared, and where decisions were made by the people closest to the work.

That approach was tested during the 2008 financial crisis. Instead of laying people off, the worker-owners collectively chose to reduce hours and share the burden. The company survived, intact in both culture and capability.

South Mountain's story shows that democratic ownership can be more than an ideal. In the right context, it can be a durable form of Evergreen stewardship.

CHOICE ONE ENGINEERING: A DIY SUCCESSION MODEL

For Matt Hoying, president of Choice One Engineering, the challenge wasn't ideology, it was practicality. The company didn't neatly fit the typical ESOP or trust model, and Hoying wasn't interested in forcing a structure that didn't suit the business.

So, they designed their own solution: what Hoying calls a DIY-SOP—a do-it-yourself succession ownership plan.

Instead of selling to an outside buyer or adopting a complex formal structure, Choice One created a homegrown ownership path that allowed leadership and ownership to transition internally over time. It required tough conversations about control, risk, and value, but it also allowed the company to preserve independence and reward the people who had helped build it.

The result wasn't a perfect template others could copy. It was something better: a model that fit the company's culture and created a clear path forward without sacrificing what made the business work.

NO TEMPLATES—ONLY TRADE-OFFS

Worker cooperatives, DIY ownership plans, and multi-shareholder LLCs won't show up on most bankers' shortlists. They require more intention, more patience, and often more humility from founders.

But for leaders focused on building Evergreen companies, that's the point.

These paths remind us that succession doesn't require a perfect structure. It requires clarity about what you're trying to protect, and the courage to design ownership around that intent.

THE COMMON THREAD

Text-Em-All, SRC, Zingerman's, Choice One, South Mountain, and the many founders experimenting with similar models, chose different structures. But they're all solving the same problem: **how to transition ownership without dismantling what made the business worth building.**

These models—ESOPs, Employee Ownership Trusts, Perpetual Purpose Trusts, worker cooperatives, multi-shareholder LLCs, and home-grown succession plans—aren't just legal tools. They're expressions of a deeper intent: to build a company designed to exist well beyond the founder(s), carry the founder story and purpose forward, and resist being absorbed by an acquisition that doesn't fit.

And there's a lot to this.

I don't pretend to be an expert in ownership structures. My goal is to widen your field of view and to show you that there's a growing world beyond the default "sell to private equity or a strategic buyer." Those conventional paths matter, and they can be the right answer in many situations. In the next chapter, we'll take a closer look at the more traditional models.

But if you're drawn to these alternative paths—if you want to preserve mojo, protect your people, and keep the founding story intact—the best way to go deeper isn't by reading another article or comparing legal diagrams. It's by getting into the right conversations.

That's one of the advantages of joining a community of business owners like The Small Giants. Many members are at the forefront of this shift in ownership. They are living these questions in real time, experimenting with different models, learning alongside specialists, and openly sharing what is working, what they have tried, and what they wish they had known sooner.

You don't need to decide on a structure yet, or even know which model might fit. What matters now is slowing down long enough to get clear on what you're trying to preserve, who you want to serve next, and what trade-offs you're willing to make.

FREEDOM FACTORS

1. OWNERSHIP IS A DESIGN CHOICE, NOT A DEFAULT

Selling to the highest bidder is one path, but not the only path. Before you decide, widen your field of view and understand the alternatives available to you.

2. STRUCTURE FOLLOWS INTENT

ESOPs, trusts, cooperatives, and custom models are tools. What matters is clarity about what you're trying to preserve: culture, independence, community, or legacy, and choosing a structure that protects it.

3. EVERY PATH INVOLVES TRADE-OFFS

There is no perfect model. Liquidity, control, continuity, and stewardship rarely maximize at the same time. The goal isn't perfection. It's alignment with your values and long-term intent.

CHAPTER 19:
Traditional Exits and Their Place in the Journey

Strategic sales, private equity partnerships, and management buyouts remain the most common ways owners transition. They're familiar, well-supported by advisors, and, done well, can convert years of sweat into real freedom.

But the "right" exit isn't only about price. It's about alignment: with your values, your legacy, your timeline, and the life you want after the deal closes. This chapter isn't a crash course in deal types. It's a practical lens for choosing the path that fits *you*.

Before you pick a path, decide what you're optimizing for: **price, speed, control, legacy, or ongoing involvement.** You won't maximize all five.

Why Traditional Exits Still Lead The Pack

Traditional exits are the default road most owners see first. They're the most familiar, the most talked about, and often perceived as the "easiest" way to unlock value—especially when you're tired, ready for change, or simply want options.

But "traditional" doesn't mean straightforward. These deals can be complex, emotional, and demanding. As we've discussed earlier, many owners aren't prepared for an exit of any kind, and a significant percentage (70 percent) of businesses that go to market never sell. That's why readiness matters. The work I've stepped you through in previous chapters isn't optional, it's essential if you want to create a business that lands in the 30 percent pool of valuable, sellable companies.

Still, strategic buyers, private equity, and management buyouts remain the most common routes because they offer three practical advantages:

1. **Market-driven valuations**

   When there are motivated buyers and a strong fit, competition can drive price and terms.

2. **Clean(er) break**

   You can usually define a clear handover period, a clear set of expectations, and a clear moment when you step away.

3. **Established processes**

   There's an ecosystem built around these exits, advisors, legal frameworks, standard steps, which makes the journey navigable, even if it isn't easy.

THREE TRADITIONAL EXIT PATHS (AT A GLANCE)

Path	What It Optimizes For	Your Role Post-Close	Typical Mechanics	Best When
Strategic Buyer	Highest price if strong synergies; preservation when values align	Shorter transition	100 percent sale, limited earnout, integration plan	You care about legacy and fit; you're comfortable stepping back
Private Equity (PE)	Accelerated growth and a second bite at the apple	Usually remain in role with earnout	Majority sale with rollover equity, board governance, bolt-ons	You want to scale, de-risk, and participate in the upside
Management Buyout (MBO)	Continuity of team, culture, customer relationships	Short transition or advisory	Bank/sponsor debt + seller financing; staged buy	You've built a ready leadership bench and value stewardship over max price

Strategic Buyers

A strategic buyer acquires your company for strategic fit, not just current earnings. They're buying customers, capabilities, IP, team, brand, and the advantage those assets give them.

Unlike financial buyers, strategic acquirers often see synergies beyond EBITDA. If there's alignment, they may value your culture, leadership model, and brand equity in ways the market multiple alone would never justify.

Best when

- You have differentiated capability, recurring revenue, or brand strength
- You want a cleaner exit (short transition, then out)
- Legacy matters, and you're willing to do diligence on *fit*, not just terms

Watch-outs

- Culture clash can erase what they paid for
- Integration risk (systems, brand, org chart)
- Earnouts can become traps when you don't control the levers post-close

CASE STUDY: BERYL HEALTH TO STERICYCLE

Recall how Paul Spiegelman walked away from a private equity deal when it became clear the buyer was focused on margin expansion over stewardship. The culture he had built at Beryl, grounded in employee engagement and long-term thinking, was too important to risk. Rather than accept misaligned terms, he chose to step back and reinvest in the business.

When Stericycle approached later, the conversation was different. Their leadership took time to understand Beryl's operating model and culture, seeing it not as a soft asset but as part of the strategic value. The deal closed at an exceptional multiple, and Spiegelman chose to step into a culture leadership role post-sale, not because he was locked into an earn-out, but because he believed alignment existed. The lesson is simple: the best strategic buyers don't just acquire earnings. They recognize and value the philosophy that produced them.

Private Equity

Private equity is rarely a "walk away" exit. It's typically a liquidity event combined with a partnership: cash today, equity rolled forward, and a mandate to grow—quickly and deliberately.

PE firms aren't just buying your current earnings. They're underwriting a future outcome. That usually means professionalized governance, sharper performance metrics, and a defined investment horizon.

Best when

- Your industry is consolidating and you can become a platform
- You have a capable leadership team and scalable operations
- You're energized by growth and willing to stay involved

Watch-outs

- Pace and performance expectations jump
- Governance becomes formal (board, reporting cadence, covenants)
- Their horizon is time-boxed (typically four to seven years), and that shapes decisions

CASE STUDY: WRENCH

Wrench, a regional HVAC services company, illustrates how private equity can accelerate a consolidation strategy.[57] When Investcorp acquired the business in 2016, Wrench was generating roughly $150 million in revenue. Its financial performance mattered, but so did its reputation for strong customer service and operational discipline.

Rather than treat Wrench as a standalone asset, Investcorp positioned it as a platform for acquiring and integrating similar businesses in a fragmented industry. Through a disciplined roll-up strategy, Wrench expanded rapidly. Investcorp ultimately exited at a significant multiple of its original investment, and the company continued growing under new ownership.

The lesson isn't that private equity is inherently better or worse. It's that PE works best when the founder wants a second chapter of growth, is comfortable with increased scrutiny, and understands that the clock is always running.

Management Buyouts (MBOs)

If you've built a strong leadership team and want to keep the business in trusted hands, a management buyout (MBO) can be a compelling path. In an MBO, your existing leaders, the people who already understand the customers, the culture, and the economics, step up as owners.

For many founders, the appeal is continuity. The business stays close to its roots. The people who helped build it have the opportunity to own it. The culture doesn't need to be reinterpreted by an outside buyer. And an MBO can be a good launch pad for broader based employee ownership.

Best when

- You've built a leadership bench ready to own, not just operate

57   Ted Billies, "Successful Private Equity Firms Manage Talent Differently," *Harvard Business Review* 5, no.12 (2024), https://hbr.org/2024/12/successful-private-equity-firms-manage-talent-differently.

- Continuity and stewardship matter more than maximizing price
- You're open to a staged transition and creative financing

Watch-outs

- Funding and structure can get complex (debt, seller financing, sponsors)
- Valuation can feel personal—so bring professionalism and advisors early
- Readiness matters: great operators aren't automatically ready owners

An MBO rarely delivers the highest headline valuation. But it can offer something different: stability, continuity, and a deliberate transfer of stewardship. For founders who care deeply about who carries the business forward, that trade-off can be worth it.

CASE STUDY: THE SRC STORY

Before SRC became one of the most well-known employee-owned companies in the world, it began with a **management buyout**.

In the early 1980s, Jack Stack and a small group of managers bought a failing International Harvester plant. At the time, this wasn't a grand experiment in employee ownership. It was a practical decision: the people who knew the business best stepped up to save it.

That decision changed how they thought. Ownership forced discipline. Cash flow mattered. Every decision had consequence. Over time, that ownership mindset expanded beyond the leadership team through open-book management and financial education. Eventually, SRC transitioned into an ESOP, broadening ownership across the organization.

A Well-Mapped Landscape—and Why That Matters

Since Bo Burlingham wrote *Finish Big*, which I highly recommend you reading, the conversation around traditional exits has matured significantly. Strategic sales, private equity transactions, and management buyouts are now well understood, well documented, and supported by a sophisticated ecosystem of advisors and capital.

That's a good thing.

You're not stepping into the unknown. There are proven playbooks. There are patterns. There are predictable mistakes.

But no structure compensates for poor preparation.

The quality of an exit is rarely determined by the deal type alone. It's determined by readiness—operational, financial, and emotional—long before bankers are hired or offers arrive.

That's where we're heading next.

Red Flags to Watch For

No matter which traditional path you explore, the same warning signs tend to appear:

1. **All earnout, little cash.** Misaligned incentives when the buyer controls the future.
2. **Over-leveraged capital structures.** No room to invest, adapt, or absorb shocks.
3. **Buyers without operating depth in your niche.** Learning curves are paid for by customers and staff.
4. **No cultural diligence.** If they don't ask about values, they won't protect them.
5. **Vague integration plans.** "We'll figure it out later" usually means your brand is at risk

How to protect your legacy:

If legacy matters to you, it needs to be designed into the process, not hoped for.

1. **Do reverse diligence.** Speak with former sellers, portfolio leaders, and customers.
2. **Codify non-negotiables.** Brand standards, people practices, customer promises—document them.
3. **Bake protection into the deal.** Governance terms, covenants, retention pools, and milestones tied to service and culture.
4. **Keep the storytellers.**Identify culture carriers and give them defined roles through transition.
5. **Prepare early.** Clean financials, clear processes, and credible reporting build trust and options.

Choosing The Right Exit—For You

At the risk of repeating myself, get clear on your expectations. Start with outcomes. Not offers.

What do you want your life to look like **six, twelve, and thirty-six months after closing**? How involved do you want to be? What are you unwilling to compromise?

Price matters. So do people, purpose, and your next chapter.

The right buyer isn't just someone who can close a deal. It's someone who can carry what you've built forward.

FREEDOM FACTORS

1. PREPARATION BUILDS NEGOTIATING STRENGTH

Regardless of deal type, buyers will assess leadership depth, financial clarity, and founder dependence. When those foundations are strong and clearly presented, trust forms early, and leverage stays in your hands when terms shift under scrutiny.

2. EVALUATE THE BUYER AS RIGOROUSLY AS THEY EVALUATE YOU

Due diligence isn't one-sided. Understand how they make decisions, how they treat operators, and whether they protect what you value. Structure can be adjusted. Misalignment cannot.

3. PROTECT YOUR OUTCOME BEFORE EMOTIONS ENTER THE ROOM

Initial offers often change once diligence begins. Know your bottom line, financially and personally, before momentum builds. Clarity prevents you from accepting a deal that compromises your next chapter.

CHAPTER 20:
Your Exit Team and Timeline

Selling your business will likely be the most significant transaction of your entrepreneurial life. It's exciting. It's complex. And it's not something you should attempt alone.

I learned that the hard way.

Even after watching other exits from the sidelines, I underestimated how different the skill set is. As owners, we're used to being the closer—the problem-solver who figures things out. But exits expose blind spots. Negotiating with experienced acquirers without the right support isn't confidence. It's stupidity.

During my own process, I found myself negotiating directly with the CEO and acquisition team of a public company. I was out of my depth. My focus shifted to "getting the deal done," and the business suffered. Over six months, momentum slipped. Revenue softened. And I came face to face with the uncomfortable truth that without me the business wouldn't thrive. Something Peter, the CEO across the table from me, picked up early on in our negotiations.

Carl Saunders learned a similar lesson.

Carl's Story: "We Thought We Could Handle It Ourselves"

Like me, Saunders and his business partner thought they'd had done the work. They'd spent years building a company they were proud of, and they had a clear valuation target in mind. When the time came to sell, they made one decision that changed everything: they chose to go without an exit team.

At first, it felt manageable. Then the process expanded, and fast. Buyer conversations multiplied. Requests piled up. Negotiations and legal documents became a second full-time job. Saunders told me it felt like doing three jobs at once: running the business, running the deal, and trying to keep everyone calm.

The business paid the price. While their attention was on the transaction, execution slipped. Revenue softened, profitability took a hit, and the company lost some of its shine at exactly the wrong moment. Buyers noticed. Confidence wobbled. The deal fell through.

Saunders's takeaway was blunt: if they'd brought in experts—an M&A advisor, an attorney, a tax strategist—the outcome would have been different. Instead, they ended up exhausted, rebuilding from a weaker position, and learning the hard way that trying to do it all yourself isn't worth the cost.

What's important is what happened next. As you read in earlier chapters, Saunders didn't stay stuck. He brought in a coach, clarified the company's purpose, and rallied the business around it. He strengthened the leadership team, reduced dependency, and rebuilt momentum. Over time, the company grew from roughly $5 million to $8 million, and beyond. And eventually, Saunders did navigate a well-deserved exit.

But it came with a price: **time.** The failed attempt didn't just cost energy, it cost years. Years of doing the work that could have been done earlier, with the right team in place, while the business was still at full strength. That's the lesson here. You can recover. You can rebuild. But it's far easier, and far less expensive, when you treat your exit like a team sport from the start.

Exiting is a Team Sport

Saunders's experience, and mine, point to the same reality: selling a business isn't something you *add* to your workload. It competes with it.

An exit process pulls attention, creates uncertainty, and introduces pressure at every level of the organization. If the founder tries to carry the deal alone, the business almost always feels it. Momentum slips. Decisions slow. Confidence wobbles. And the very value you're trying to realize starts to erode.

That's why exits work best when they're treated like a team sport.

Your role as the owner is not to negotiate every clause or manage every conversation. Your job is to keep the business strong, the leadership aligned, and the narrative consistent while others handle the mechanics of the deal.

The right exit team does three things simultaneously:

- **Protects value** while the business continues to operate at full strength
- **Reduces risk** by anticipating issues before they surface in diligence
- **Preserves optionality**, so you're choosing from positions of strength, not reacting under pressure

Without that support, founders often become the bottleneck, pulled into every decision, distracted by every request, and stretched across too many roles at once.

With the right team in place, something important shifts. You stop *running a sale* and start *leading a business through a transition*. That distinction is what separates stressful exits from successful ones.

The question isn't whether you can do parts of this yourself. It's whether you should.

Your Exit Roster: Who Protects What

A strong exit team is small, experienced, and clear on roles. Each protects a different dimension of the outcome.

M&A Advisor—Protects Value

Runs the process, creates competitive tension, and prevents you from negotiating against yourself.

M&A Attorney—Protects Risk

Manages structure, representations, warranties, earnouts, and post-close obligations.

Tax Strategist—Protects Proceeds

Ensures you don't win on valuation and lose after tax.

Wealth Advisor—Protects Your Future

Translates liquidity into a plan aligned with your next chapter.

Coach or Trusted Guide—Protects Perspective

Keeps you grounded when identity, control, and emotion surface.

Your job isn't to master these disciplines. It's to assemble them early enough that they can do theirs.

A NOTE ON DEAL SIZE AND ROLES

The shape of your exit team will vary with the size and complexity of your deal.

In smaller transactions, a seasoned **business broker** may play the role of M&A advisor, supported by a strong attorney and tax specialist. In larger or more complex exits, that role is typically filled by a dedicated **M&A or investment banking team**, often with additional specialists layered in.

The titles matter less than the expertise. What's essential, at any size, is that you work with an experienced team—people who understand your goals—and can help you navigate an exit successfully.

The biggest risk isn't having a "lightweight" team. It's relying on generalists, or assuming you can fill the gaps yourself.

The Exit Timeline: Four Phases That Protect Value

Who you involve matters, but **when** you involve them matters just as much.

Most owners think of an exit as an event. In reality, it's a progression. And the biggest difference between a clean exit and a painful one is whether you're preparing from a position of strength or reacting under pressure.

Here are four phases to think about. The dates will vary by business, but the sequence holds.

PHASE 1: BUILD READINESS (18 TO 36 MONTHS OUT)

This is where leverage is created.

At this stage, you're not selling. You're strengthening the business so that, when the time comes, it stands on its own.

That means reducing owner dependency. Deepening leadership capability. Cleaning up financial reporting. Addressing customer or supplier concentration. Tightening execution rhythm so performance is consistent and predictable.

From the outside, you want a business that is understandable, transferable, and resilient.

This is also personal preparation. Letting go doesn't happen at closing, it starts here. A coach or trusted advisor can help you separate identity from role and prepare emotionally for what's ahead.

Tax planning also belongs in this phase. Once a deal is live, most structuring flexibility disappears.

Early readiness expands your options. Late readiness narrows them.

PHASE 2: DE-RISK THE DEAL (9 TO 18 MONTHS OUT)

This phase is about eliminating surprises before they surface in diligence.

Buyers rarely walk away because they dislike the business. They walk away because they discover uncertainty—messy contracts, unclear intellectual property ownership, inconsistent reporting, undocumented processes, unresolved liabilities.

Now you begin thinking like a buyer before one is in the room.

Your M&A attorney and tax strategist help tighten documentation, clarify ownership, address structural weaknesses, and prepare the business for scrutiny.

You're still not "selling." You're strengthening the foundation so that when scrutiny comes, it doesn't destabilize confidence.

Confidence preserves value. Uncertainty erodes it.

PHASE 3: GO TO MARKET (3 TO 12 MONTHS OUT)

This is where process creates options.

Now the work becomes market-facing: positioning, targeting the right buyer types, creating competitive tension, and managing the flow of information. This is when your M&A advisor (or broker, depending on deal size) earns their keep—running a structured process so you don't end up negotiating in the dark with a single party.

Your role in this phase is not to chase every conversation. It's to keep the business steady, keep leadership aligned, and ensure performance doesn't dip. The team runs the process. You lead the company.

PHASE 4: CLOSE AND TRANSITION (0 TO 3 MONTHS OUT)

This is where discipline matters.

This phase is paperwork-heavy, emotionally charged, and full of last-minute complexity. Diligence intensifies. Terms tighten. Everyone wants answers now. Your attorney is central here, protecting you from rushed concessions and ensuring what you agreed in principle survives into the final documents.

It's also when the "human deal" becomes visible: transition planning, communication, retention of key people, and protecting the founder story during the handoff. This is where a wealth advisor can help shift your attention from "closing the deal" to "building the next chapter."

THE POINT OF THE TIMELINE

This isn't about perfect planning. It's about avoiding the trap Saunders fell (and I) fell into: trying to assemble the team in the middle of the game.

When you build readiness early, you gain choices.
When you delay, you inherit pressure.

FREEDOM FACTORS

1. DON'T RUN THE DEAL AND THE BUSINESS ALONE

An exit competes with operations. If you try to manage both, performance suffers. Your role is to lead the company—not carry the transaction.

2. BUILD YOUR EXIT TEAM BEFORE YOU NEED THEM

Value, risk, proceeds, and perspective all require specialists. Assemble experienced advisors early so preparation happens from strength, not urgency.

3. CREATE LEVERAGE THROUGH TIME

Exits succeed when readiness precedes process. The earlier you build leadership depth, financial clarity, and structural resilience, the more options you retain when the market arrives.

CHAPTER 21:
Life After Exiting

Many founders think the toughest part of selling is getting the deal done. That's only true if you're prepared for what comes next. If you've taken the time to design, the next chapter intentionally.

I hadn't.

When I eventually sold my business, the post-exit picture wasn't nearly as clean as I'd imagined. My group consisted of three core businesses: a document storage company, a software company, and a queue management business. In the end, I chose a management buyout. Two members of my leadership team took over the document storage and software businesses, and another partner bought my shares in the queue management company.

But this wasn't a calm, well-orchestrated transition.

We had pulled back from a strategic acquirer and brought in a coach to help us implement The Great Game of Business®. In my mind, we were regrouping. The truth? My heart wasn't in it anymore. I was exhausted.

I had entered negotiations without an exit team. I had let the process drag on. We had even moved out of our warehouse and into the acquirer's facility—more space, more flexibility, better infrastructure. But it left me exposed. They had the leverage, and I was in a half-pregnant situation. Not sold, not independent.

So, I pulled the ejection cord.

I sat down with my accountant and valued the businesses. Then I offered them to key people on my management team. We structured payments over five years, funded out of future profits. It was a risk I convinced myself I was comfortable taking. At the time, I was living halfway across the world, my marriage was on the rocks, I was distracted by a new venture, and if I'm honest, I was in self-destruct mode. Clean structure wasn't my priority. Escape was.

In the end, the contracts were never fully honored. Both businesses ran into trouble—partly due to the South African economy, but not only because of that. My leadership team, good people though they were, didn't yet have the experience to take the companies to the next level.

The result wasn't catastrophe. But it wasn't freedom either. I poured everything into a new venture in a foreign country... over indexing on a single purpose again. I didn't bring my A-game to the new business. It failed. And it cost a fortune.

The experience left me financially ruined and emotionally broken. And that brings me full circle to why I wrote this book.

Entrepreneurship is a calling. We feel compelled to create something from nothing. It's hard work to build a viable business. It's even harder to sustain it and scale it.

But the hardest part is learning how to transition on our own terms.

Most entrepreneurs receive no formal training in how to run a business, let alone how to sell one or step away from one. We learn by doing. We learn by surviving. And sometimes, we learn the expensive way.

My hope is that the stories in this book spare you some of that cost. That they encourage you to seek the right help, build the right support, and prepare intentionally, wherever you are along your journey.

Research frequently cited in the exit-planning world suggests that **around three-quarters of business owners experience some form of profound regret within a year of selling**.[58] The number varies by study and definition, but the pattern is consistent: it's common for owners to feel unsettled after an exit, sometimes surprisingly so.

---

58   The Exit Planning Institute, *2023 National State of Owner Readiness Report,* https://exit-planning-institute.org/state-of-owner-readiness, accessed January 2025.

That regret doesn't necessarily mean selling was "wrong."

It usually means the owner was unprepared for what the sale would take with it.

Because selling a business is not only a transaction. It's a transition. And transitions are identity events.

This is the part most exit conversations skip. They obsess over valuation, deal structure, tax strategy, earn-outs, and handovers. Those are important. But if you treat the human side of the exit like an afterthought, you can end up with a "successful" sale… and a deeply unsatisfying life.

I wrote this book for one reason: to make sure you don't reach the end of the road and realize you built a business yet forgot to build a valuable life.

For me, my business was the primary container for my purpose. I justified it (and sometimes still do) by convincing myself that the work I do is what makes everything else in my life possible. And that work becomes my sole purpose to the detriment of everything else in my life.

And that's where the danger is.

We humans have many purposes across a lifetime. The problem for entrepreneurs is that we tend to over-index on one purpose, the business, until it crowds out everything else.

Then the exit happens, and the purpose collapses overnight.

The outcome isn't just boredom. It can be grief. It can be disorientation. It can be a quiet sense of, *"If I'm not that person anymore… who am I?"*

If you've built your identity around being the founder, the CEO, the fixer, the rainmaker, the final decision-maker, exiting doesn't just remove your job. It removes the mirror you've been using to understand yourself.

Many entrepreneurs hit the exit with one foot out the door, desperate to be done, but strangely unable to imagine what "done" looks like. They don't just want to escape what they've created.

They want to leave exhaustion.
They want to leave pressure.
They want to leave the weight of being the one holding it all together.

And I get that. But if you haven't done the deeper work—if you haven't separated *who you are* from *what you built*—the exit can create a vacuum that money won't fill.

THE QUIET AFTER THE CELEBRATION

There is a moment after an exit that few people describe honestly. The documents are signed. The lawyers step back. The intensity that has carried you for months begins to fade. Congratulations arrive and for a while there is relief. It feels like you have crossed a finish line.

Then you look at your calendar.

For the first time in years, sometimes decades, your schedule isn't full because the business needs you. There is space where urgency used to live. If you are not prepared for that moment, the silence can feel unfamiliar and, at times, unsettling.

Bo Burlingham writes in *Finish Big* that leaving well is deeply personal. It is not only about price.[59] It requires intention, emotional preparation, and clarity about what matters next, not just what you are stepping away from.

I have seen owners respond to this new space in predictable ways. Some start another business almost immediately, not always intentionally, but more often from discomfort. Others throw themselves into investing or advisory roles simply to stay occupied. Some spend money quickly. Some say yes to everything. And some drift quietly, wondering why the freedom they worked so hard for does not feel the way they imagined.

The reality is that the goal was never simply to exit. The goal was to create choice. A valuable business is only half the equation. The other half is a meaningful after.

---

59   Burlingham, *Finish Big.*

If that second half has not been considered before the sale, it is difficult to design it well once the noise has stopped.

WHY COMMUNITY MATTERS MORE THAN MOST OWNERS REALIZE

One of the healthiest things you can do long before a sale is to widen your circle.

Exit planning usually begins with accountants, attorneys, and bankers. Those conversations are necessary. But they are not sufficient. There is another layer that matters just as much. It is the layer where you speak with people who have already walked through the identity shift that follows a transition.

Most owners prepare financially and legally, yet avoid the deeper conversations about purpose, relevance, and what comes next. They keep those thoughts private. They assume they will sort them out later.

This is one of the reasons communities like Small Giants matter in the context of succession and transition. They bring together values-driven leaders who care not only about building great companies, but about living meaningful lives. In those environments, business owners can get vulnerable and talk about the softer side of a transition.

If you have carried responsibility alone for years, the transition is not the moment to continue doing so.

Build relational support before you need it. Join a peer group. Spend time with leaders who are ahead of you on the path. Not because something is wrong, but because you are preparing well. When you are surrounded by people who have navigated these waters, the transition becomes less dramatic and more intentional.

Community does not eliminate uncertainty. It simply makes it shared.

The Emotional Reality of Letting Go

Most owners prepare for the legal and financial parts of an exit. Far fewer prepare for the human side.

Letting go of a business you built isn't like leaving a job. Over time, the company becomes more than work, it becomes a place where you feel useful, connected, and in control of outcomes. It gives structure to your days and meaning to your effort. When you step away, you don't just change what you do; you change the role the business has been playing in your life.

That's why an exit can produce unexpected emotion, even when it's the right decision and even when the outcome is positive.

Again, Burlingham captures this bluntly in *Finish Big*: leaving a company well is often harder than starting one.[60] Starting is full of possibility. Exiting contains endings. Routines end. Relationships change. A version of you retires.

That does not mean something is wrong. It means something significant has shifted.

Many founders are surprised by how layered the emotion can be. Relief can sit next to sadness. Pride can sit next to doubt. Excitement can sit next to restlessness. This is why being part of a community of business owners who have been there and who genuinely care is so important.

WHY IT CAN FEEL LIKE LOSS (EVEN WHEN IT'S A WIN)

Many founders are surprised by the "after," because the business has been carrying more than financial weight. Davin Salvagno's point is useful here: humans often have multiple purposes across a lifetime, but entrepreneurs can over-invest purpose into one container, the business. When that container is removed quickly, the void can feel larger than expected.

---

60   Burlingham, *Finish Big*.

When the container is removed quickly, the void can feel larger than expected. Recall James Ashford. After his exit, despite the headlines and the congratulations, he found himself curled up on the pavement outside his home, overwhelmed and disoriented. Nothing dramatic had happened that day. There was no crisis. But the intensity that had shaped his identity for years had vanished, along with the structure and certainty it had provided. The deal had been phenomenal. The outcome was objectively brilliant. Yet the sudden absence of purpose left him shaken, face to face with a silence he had never learned how to navigate.

For years, you've likely been "the one"—the final decision-maker, the problem-solver, the person carrying responsibility. Even if you've built a strong leadership team, that identity can be deeply embedded. Exiting forces a new story: you're no longer central to the system you built.

That shift can surface emotions that feel contradictory: relief and sadness, pride and grief, excitement and uncertainty. It can also create restlessness, especially in the first months, because your days are suddenly quieter and your sense of relevance is no longer automatically reinforced.

If you treat the emotional transition as an afterthought, you may rush into the next thing simply to escape that discomfort. That's where many owners make avoidable mistakes.

PREPARING BEFORE YOU STEP AWAY

You cannot eliminate emotion from a transition. But you can soften the shock.

Start by noticing what the business gives you beyond money. It may give you structure. Status. Challenge. Belonging. Control. A sense of momentum. When you name those elements, you can begin to cultivate them elsewhere.

Second, build the bridge before you need it. Mentor while you are still running the company. Join a board. Invest time in community leadership.

Deepen relationships. Redistribute your sense of purpose before the business changes shape.

Third, surround yourself with people who understand the terrain. A coach. A peer group. A values-driven community. These are not luxuries. They are stabilizers.

Finally, allow yourself space after the transaction. Do not rush to fill every hour. The nervous system needs time to recalibrate. Clarity rarely arrives in the middle of intensity.

Exiting well is not only about maximizing price. It is about ensuring that what follows feels aligned with the freedom you were seeking in the first place.

Purpose After the Exit

I hope that by now, you know how important it is to think about your purpose and what's next with some intention.

For many owners, the challenge isn't a lack of options. It's figuring out which of those options fit with your purpose. The goal isn't to "stay busy." It's to **be intentional about what's next in a broader, healthier way** than the business alone could ever provide.

A practical way to start is to ask three simple questions:

- **What have I neglected that matters to me?** (relationships, health, learning, creativity, community)
- **Where do I still want to contribute?** (mentoring, building, teaching, investing, leading)
- **What does "enough" look like now?** (time, intensity, responsibility, lifestyle)

From there, most owners find themselves drawn to one (or a combination) of the following paths:

1. **Mentor and develop others**

    Some of the most satisfying "next chapters" are built around passing on hard-won lessons—through mentoring, coaching emerging leaders, supporting founders, or investing time in leadership development. Jack Stack is a great example of an owner who continued contributing by teaching and supporting other businesses after stepping back.

2. **Stay close to business—without carrying the weight**

    Many entrepreneurs don't retire well because they don't actually want to stop building—they want to stop being trapped. Advisory work, board roles, and strategic projects can give you the stimulation of business without pulling you back into the operational grind.

3. **Invest with intention**

    Angel investing, search funds, or backing purpose-aligned companies can be deeply rewarding, especially when you bring more than money. The difference between "investing as a distraction" and "investing as a purpose" is whether you're clear on what you're trying to build in this next phase.

4. **Build something new (for the right reasons)**

    Some owners will start another venture. That can be energizing, if it comes from clarity and desire, not from discomfort with stillness. A useful rule: if you're starting something primarily to avoid the emotional quiet after an exit, pause. If you're starting because you've found a compelling mission and you're genuinely ready, it can be a powerful reinvention.

Whatever path you choose, remember this: **you don't need the business to be your only "why" anymore.** In fact, you're better off if it isn't. The next chapter works best when purpose is distributed across relationships, contribution, learning, health, community, and meaningful work.

This is also where community matters. Exit and succession can be strangely isolating, especially if the people around you haven't been through it. Staying connected to other values-driven owners—through peer groups, circles, or the Small Giants Community—keeps you grounded, gives you perspective, and helps you shape your next chapter with intention rather than reaction.

You may step away from running a business day-to-day, but if you're an entrepreneur at heart, you won't stop creating. The goal is to **choose what you build next**, and to build it in a way that supports the freedom you set out to create in the first place.

Managing the Financial Windfall

One of the most persistent myths about exiting a business is that once the money arrives, everything else sorts itself out.

It doesn't.

For many owners, managing a significant liquidity event is unfamiliar territory. You've spent years allocating capital inside a business—investing in people, growth, systems, and strategy. Post-exit, the challenge shifts from building value to preserving and deploying it wisely.

That shift deserves just as much intention as the exit itself.

Former CEOs and founders often underestimate this transition. Research into post-exit outcomes shows that many struggle not because they lack resources,[61] but because they suddenly face decisions they've never had to make before—across taxes, investments, risk tolerance, and lifestyle design. Treat this phase as a new discipline to learn, not something to outsource blindly.

A few principles matter more than tactics:

First, slow the money down. Unless there's a compelling reason, avoid major financial decisions immediately after an exit. Give yourself time

---

61   Randy T. Byrnes and Scott N. Taylor, "Voluntary Transition of the CEO: Owner CEOs' Sense of Self Before, During, and After Transition," *Frontiers in Psychology* 27, no. 10 (2015) https://www.frontiersin.org/journals/psychology/articles/10.3389/fpsyg.2015.01633/full.

to decompress emotionally before committing capital. Clarity improves dramatically once the nervous system settles.

Second, assemble the right advisory bench. This isn't about finding one "smart" advisor. It's about building a small, coordinated team—typically a wealth advisor, tax specialist, and estate planner—who understand your goals and communicate well with each other. The quality of this team will shape outcomes for decades.

Third, align the money with your values and life design. The purpose of the windfall isn't accumulation for its own sake. It's optionality. Freedom. The ability to choose how you spend your time, energy, and attention. That means being explicit about what you want the money *to do* for you—security, simplicity, contribution, growth, legacy, or a mix of all five.

Finally, separate identity from net worth. It's easy—quietly—to start measuring success in a new way after an exit. Resist that. The money is a tool, not a scorecard. If you don't define "enough," the number will keep moving, and freedom will remain just out of reach.

Handled well, the financial windfall doesn't complicate your life—it stabilizes it. It creates space for better decisions, healthier rhythms, and a next chapter built on choice rather than pressure.

FREEDOM FACTORS

1. AN EXIT IS A TRANSITION, NOT A TRANSACTION

Price, structure, and tax matter. But what determines whether you feel free afterward is whether you prepared for the identity shift. If you do not design the life beyond the business before the sale, the silence after closing can feel heavier than expected.

2. FREEDOM AFTER EXIT IS BUILT IN COMMUNITY

Advisors prepare you for the deal. Peers prepare you for the transition. Surround yourself with values driven leaders who understand succession, identity, and reinvention. Shared perspective stabilizes uncertainty and makes the next chapter intentional rather than reactive.

3. IF THE BUSINESS IS YOUR ONLY PURPOSE, THE EXIT WILL FEEL LIKE LOSS

Over time, your company becomes more than income. It becomes identity, structure, relevance, and community. When that container changes, the void can feel disorienting. Redistribute purpose before you step away so freedom expands rather than contracts.

CONCLUSION:
Crafting a Legacy of Freedom and Purpose

This book was never about building a bigger business.

It was about building a business that gives you your life back, without losing the meaning that made you start in the first place.

If there's one idea, I hope you carry forward, it's this: **freedom doesn't arrive at the end of the journey. Freedom is designed through intentional decision making and alignment with your goals.** Designed through clarity of purpose, disciplined leadership, a team that can carry the load, and a company built to create value without consuming you.

Over these chapters, the work has followed a simple arc:

1. OWN YOUR ROLE AS THE LEADER

At some point, every founder meets the same crossroads: keep being the hero or become the owner. The operator mindset builds momentum early. The owner mindset builds a company that can last. That shift isn't tactical, it's personal. It requires letting go of control, building decision-making depth, and choosing leadership over rescue.

2. BUILD WITH INTENTION

Growth without intent is a trap. It feels like progress, but it often produces complexity, exhaustion, and a business that relies increasingly on you. Intentional growth starts with purpose and values, and then aligns strategy, execution, and priorities to match. That's how you create momentum that doesn't come at the cost of your health, relationships, or peace of mind.

3. CREATE VALUE THAT BUYS FREEDOM

A valuable company is one that can perform without the founder at the center. It serves a clear core customer. It is differentiated. It generates predictable cash. It has systems and leaders that reduce dependency on you as the single point of failure. When those elements are in place, the business becomes an asset, not a machine that needs feeding.

4. TREAT SUCCESSION AS STEWARDSHIP

Succession isn't the end. It's the handoff of something you've built with care—people, culture, customers, and a legacy that matters. Whether you sell, recap, transition to the next generation, or move toward employee ownership, the question isn't just "How do I exit?" It's "How do I pass this on well?"

A FINAL INVITATION

You don't have to do this alone.

The business owners and leaders I work with surround themselves with other leaders who care about building great companies and living great lives—people who understand the weight of leadership, the complexity of succession, and the importance of purpose.

That's what the Small Giants Community exists for. It's a place for leaders who choose to be great over being big, to learn, to connect, and to keep growing into the kind of stewardship this book has been pointing toward. If this book resonated, you'll find your people there.

Gratitude

Thank you to my partner, Sinem Dörter, for the unwavering support you have given me over the past few years. Writing this book and stepping into the leadership of the Small Giants Community has been a meaningful journey, but not always an easy one. Your encouragement, patience, and belief in what I'm building have meant more than I can put into words.

Thank you to the many guests and friends who joined me on *The Freedom Experience* podcast. Your stories, insights, and willingness to share openly are what truly bring this book to life. Without your voices and experiences, these pages would not carry the same meaning.

I'm deeply grateful to those who invested their time as first readers of this manuscript. Your thoughtful feedback, encouragement, and honest reflections helped shape this book in ways that made it far stronger than it would have been otherwise.

Thank you to Bo Burlingham and Paul Spiegelman for the extraordinary impact you have had on the entrepreneurial world. Bo, through the remarkable books you've written and the ideas you've championed. Paul, for making the Small Giants Community possible and for creating a movement that continues to inspire leaders to build businesses that are great, not just big.

And to my family, thank you for your love and encouragement throughout this journey. Your support has been a constant source of strength.

Finally, I want to acknowledge my father, whose belief in me continues to guide me in life and beyond. His influence and encouragement helped make this moment possible.

About the Author

 Jean Moncrieff is a serial entrepreneur, investor, and leadership team coach with more than three decades of experience building, scaling, and exiting businesses. Originally from South Africa, Jean started his first company as a teenager, launching a computer hardware business at the age of nineteen. Over the following years, he helped build and raise capital for one of the early web content management platforms and went on to found, finance, and exit several companies across different industries.

Having experienced the full journey of entrepreneurship—from founder and operator to investor and exit—Jean developed a deep understanding of the challenges business owners face as their companies grow. After scaling an eight-figure company that left him trapped inside the business, he spent two years transforming it into a valuable, scalable asset before successfully exiting. That experience reshaped the way he approaches business and leadership.

Today, Jean works with CEOs and leadership teams to build valuable companies that can grow without consuming their lives. He is the founder of Emerge Accelerators and leads the Small Giants Community, a global network of purpose-driven business owners committed to building companies that are great rather than simply big.

Jean splits his time between Switzerland and the United States, where he continues to work with founders and leadership teams around the world.

DISCOVER THE SMALL GIANTS COMMUNITY

The Small Giants Community is a global network of purpose-driven entrepreneurs who believe a business can be both successful and deeply meaningful. Inspired by Bo Burlingham's book *Small Giants*, the community brings together leaders who choose to build companies that are **great instead of simply big.**

Members of the Small Giants Community are committed to creating exceptional cultures, developing their people, and making a positive impact on the communities they serve. Through events, learning experiences, and deep peer relationships, the community creates a space where leaders can challenge conventional thinking about growth and success.

If you believe business can be a force for good—and that purpose, people, and culture matter just as much as profit—the Small Giants Community is where you'll find your peers.

Learn more at **SmallGiants.org**.

BOOK JEAN MONCRIEFF
TO SPEAK WITH YOUR TEAM, PROGRAM, OR ORGANIZATION

Jean is represented by the Gray | Miller Agency, a leading speaking firm comprised of the world's most diverse, engaging, and influential speakers, authors, and thought leaders.

For speaking inquiries, please visit **GrayMillerAgency.com** or submit a request at **JeanMoncrieff.com**.

Representing a community of authors whose books have collectively sold hundreds of millions of copies, the founders of The Gray + Miller Agency launched Maison Vero, a professional publishing house that partners with rising authors to bring their thought leadership to the world. Our representation covers every aspect of thought leadership, including U.S. senators, governors, and ambassadors, billionaire founders and entrepreneurs, researchers, academics, scientists, consultants, practitioners, social influencers, C-suite leaders, adventurers, professional athletes, artists, and creators. We partner with thought leaders and world changers like you who have a story to tell. By bringing decades of professional expertise to our clients, we are charting a new path in a timeless industry that transcends publishing norms, transforming powerful thoughts into impactful books that inspire minds, ignite hearts, and open doors.

Visit maisonvero.com to view our growing list of authors, or to submit a proposal for publication consideration.

Follow Maison Vero for insight and inspiration on social media:

 MaisonVero    MaisonVero    MaisonVeroPublishing

For information about special discounts for bulk purchases, please call 1-949-333-4872 or email info@graymilleragency.com.

Maison Vero is a partner brand of The Gray + Miller Agency, a speaking, literary, and talent consortium. For more information on the talent represented by The Gray + Miller Agency, or to bring any of our thought leaders to your organization or live event, please visit our website at **graymilleragency.com**.